# FROM LIMITATION AND FEAR TO VASTNESS AND PEACE

*The Adventure of Coming Slowly and Suddenly to Life*

## *Hamilton Salsich*

(with special thanks to my children,
grandchildren, siblings, colleagues, friends,
and *especially* my beloved wife, Delycia)

Plain and Simple Press
Mystic, CT
2016

ISBN: 0692771662
ISBN 13: 9780692771662

# CONTENTS

# INTRODUCTION

S eeing the sunlight each morning, noticing that darkness has
left the land somehow newer and fresher than before, I sometimes have the feeling of being alive all over again. I guess sleep is,
in a way, a short-lived dying-out of life, a sort of simulated death,
and so waking each morning is a kind of rebirth. With each new
dawn comes a start-over, a fresh beginning, a resurrection of ourselves, you might say. And actually, almost everything starts over in
the morning. Things clean and clear begin each day in the natural
world – some new kinds of light, the somehow youthful look of
even old snow, the crisp onsets of brand new breezes. Nothing is
old in the morning. The earth, the universe itself, is a refurbished
wonder when I awake,

I've been trying to see this newness all my life – not only the
newness of each morning, but the newness that's everywhere and
never ends, the newness that springs up inside our fresh and endless universe at every instant. It's been a challenging quest for me.
The apparent sameness of routine has plagued me for years, making newness not an easy thing to discover. In a way, I've had to be
an explorer – an easy-going but fervent voyager in the search for
the shine and sparkle of newness.

What follows are a collection of thoughts typed out on my
laptop -- impressions, intuitions, hunches, and inklings. They came

to me over 40+ years along the path of this arduous but sweet-tempered crusade of the spirit, and I wrote them in the sincerest way I know. Rather than formal writings, these are simply un-ceremonious and honest notes written along the trail by a mild-mannered warrior in the peaceful endeavor to see the lights in the everyday splendor of life.

# A SPLENDID LIFE

I hope these words don't sound too boastful, but I believe my life is a splendid one. Of course, it's the same splendor that exists in every person I pass in the grocery store, every shaft of sunshine, every shade of color on winter days, and every ripple in the Mystic River. This entire universe is an endless display of splendor, and since we're all part of the universe, we all share in the splendor. Somehow, all over the earth, billions of lungs keep lifting and falling with splendid evenness, and hearts keep helping people and panthers and butterflies stay strong in splendid ways. Just the fact that I can carry my teacup to my lips is a magnificent accomplishment, given the countless nerves and muscles that must flawlessly function together in the process. When birds wander above the river, they do it with smoothness and majesty, and when the girl greets me at the grocery checkout, her smile is a miracle to me. All of us – people, small stones on the shore, flames in a winter fireplace – share in the splendor of this earth that somehow and miraculously became our home.

## A WHATEVER KIND OF GUY

One day, visiting my grandchildren at their house in the country-side, I started messing around with some small stones on one of the many stone walls on the property – just seeing what structure I could create in a few minutes. I had no design in mind, only the desire to do something spontaneous and set the stones wherever my hands wished them to be. If someone had asked me what I was building, I might have said "whatever my hands wish" – or maybe, like so many young people today, just "whatever", perhaps with a suitable shrug. However, there would be no spirit of indifference or exasperation in my "whatever", as there often seems to be when I hear the word spoken. If I said "whatever", it would be because whatever I build with those small stones would be something special to me. I guess, in a way, I'm a whatever kind of guy. Whatever a day brings, I try to see what it has that can help me. I know that whatever happens a minute from now is the truth for that moment, and whatever thought I have at any moment helps me, somehow, be exactly who I'm supposed to be. It's a good word for me. I'm more likely to smile than shrug when I say "whatever".

---

## DINNER FOR FEAR

Like many of us, I've been fighting fear for most of my life, but now, in my 70s, I see that I probably should have been giving it a good-natured "hello", and perhaps even setting out dinner for it. Strangely, my resistance to fear has only seemed to enable it to spread and grow stronger. The more I've fought to push fear out, the more powerful it seemed to become. So, I guess I'm tossing in the towel. I'm sending up the ceasefire flag so fear can see I'm not afraid of it. In fact, I've started putting out invitations: "Please come in, fear. I'll set out dinner for you. Let's relax and learn about each other. Linger as long as you want." Fear, I'm finding, often disappears fairly soon in the face of simple hospitality.

＝≒╪╞═

## ACTUALLY DANCING

On any given day, my thoughts are usually as gossamer and scattered as the dusting of snow across Mystic some winter mornings, and that's exactly what I love most about them. I feel fortunate that my thoughts are as insubstantial as the snowflakes that floated down on us last night. Even worrisome thoughts seem to easily scatter through my mind, and, if I let them, just as easily disappear, as will this wispy sheet of snow by the afternoon. When I step back and simply observe them, I see that my thoughts are actually flimsy specks that fling themselves around in fairly disorderly ways. It's like they're having fun, these sometimes bothersome but always free-spirited thoughts that dance around inside me, and I often have fun observing them in their escapades. Like snowflakes, even the most fearful thoughts sooner or later settle to a stop -- sometimes on a computer screen in curious rows called sentences.

＝≒╪╞═

## A GRATEFUL HEART

An old church hymn asks for "a grateful heart that loves and blesses all", and this morning I'm giving some thought to the word "all". The hymn doesn't say "blesses some", or "blesses the good things that happen", or "blesses people who act the way I think they should act". It says "all", as in everything that happens, everything that comes my way – the pleasant and the unpleasant, the advantageous and the seemingly useless, the triumphs and the trouncings. The hymn suggests that every aspect of my life should somehow be honored. I should, in some way or other, bless everything that happens. As Shakespeare reminds us, blessings (he uses the word "mercy") should not be "strained", but should be shared the way "the gentle rain of heaven" falls upon the earth -- *indiscriminately, unconditionally, thoroughly*. Rain falls on the bad and the beautiful, and so should my gratitude.

---

## ABEYANCE

If the word "abeyance" means temporary inactivity, as one dictionary says, then I'm a believer in abeyance. I'd like to hold everything in abeyance about every two hours, at least – just breathing in and out for a few minutes and letting the planet spin where it will without me moving a muscle or thinking a thought. We have a stone wall in our backyard, and it strikes me with almost a sense of envy that the stones are *always* in abeyance. They simply sit in silence where they have for probably several hundred years, doing nothing but being proper stones. As I'm writing this by the window, I can see the stones outside. They're not restless, not checking off a list, not flying from one activity to the next. No, I like to think they're holding restlessness and frenzy in abeyance. The world and my life look quite peaceful when I watch those stones. In fact, I've decided to do just that for the next few minutes. I'm holding this writing in abeyance. Back later . . . maybe.

---

## SHADOWS AND WORRIES

Driving on the interstate with Delycia this morning, I started wishing that I could pass through my concerns and worries as smoothly as we passed through the many shadows of trees across the road. Even the most worrisome thoughts have no more solidity than shadows. They are like wispy winds of the mind, having less substance and shape than breezes blowing across lawns. The worries that wander into my life would wander right out again if I saw them for what they are – flimsy and frail mental shapes, no stronger than shadows across the interstate.

⊷ ⊶

## A LOYAL FOLLOWER

Goodness is a steady and faithful follower. It seems to pursue me everywhere – in stores, where I can always see a gracious smile from at least one person; on walks, where strangers usually send a greeting with a wave; and especially in the midst of disappointment and sadness, when I can always count on goodness somehow giving me its gifts. Even in disaster and desolation, goodness is persistent and enduring, a devoted follower . It's always just behind me, waiting and ready.

⊷ ⊶

## SMOOTH MOVES

Coming off the interstate this morning, I noticed the smooth flow of cars moving on and off the highway, and it started me thinking about the predominance of smooth movements all across the world – the kind of movements that seldom make the evening news. These cars, for instance, were evenly streaming around the clover leaf, as they do 24/7 all year long, with only an occasional disruption. And it happens all across the world on interstates and ramps from San Francisco to Istanbul – billions of cars smoothly cruising along with a silky kind of ease and efficiency. The same is true of pedestrian traffic, the countless walkers who work their way effortlessly along streets and sidewalks, a ceaseless and almost graceful pedestrian river. Of course, there are jostles and disruptions now and then, but mostly the worldwide stream of walkers just keeps fluidly moving. If I could somehow see all this unruffled flow of vehicles and pedestrians from a few miles above the earth, I'm sure I would think this planet was a safe and stylish place to live. Unfortunately, the evening news seldom highlights the gracefulness that's all around us. I guess the relatively scarce instances of disturbance and disarray tell a more stimulating story, but they don't tell the truth about the overall smoothness of this life we lead together on earth.

# A LUCKY LEARNER

I t's always a pleasure to attend a "workshop" of some sort – a chance to dust off some old skills or discover new ones – but no structured workshop is any better than the unrehearsed seminars presented to me day by day. In a way, all the hours and minutes are my teachers, and each separate experience creates a classroom. A quiet moment as I make my breakfast could bring new knowledge to brighten my life, and a short walk with my wife around her prospering spring gardens could give me a better understanding of myself. Even setting out my clothes for the coming day, or shifting my chair as I choose what words to type next, or driving my car in the sunlight of a new morning, or simply standing in a store beside bins of apples and pears, can provide opportunities for fresh insights. Teachers are teaching me everywhere. If I spent some time quietly looking at it, the tree that towers over our house would probably share wisdom I could use in some way, and people I pass today could tell me stories more instructive and inspiring than textbooks. I am a lucky learner in a classroom with no walls.

## CALM SPEED

As I'm slowly waking up in the morning, I often listen for a few moments to the sounds of cars speeding along the distant interstate, and, for some reason, the awareness of the speed out there seems to pleasantly increase my feeling of sleepiness and peace. The swiftness of the cars seems to be a serene swiftness, a quiet kind of speed, a lazy and lovely quickness. It starts me thinking, often, about how speedy the entire universe actually is, and how its speed is scarcely noticeable. While I am writing this in a calm and silent room, the cells in my body are doing their intricate work at dizzying speeds, and thoughts are coursing through my mind like cars on highways. As I type these words, people by the billions are dashing around the earth, and all day long, even in my coolest, most unruffled moments, the planet I live on will be spinning at 1,000 miles per hour and racing around the sun at 64,000 miles per hour. Truly, when we're sipping our morning tea in the peaceful house we share, Cia and I are two serene friends surrounded by inconceivably swift and stylish speed.

✦ ✦

## A RIVER, NOT A BATTLEFIELD

I've been battling a problem for the past few days, but I'm slowly starting to see that it's not actually a problem, and definitely doesn't require a battle. I'm disappointed in myself, because it occurs to me that I've been responding to this so-called problem in pretty much the same way I handled problems when I was 12 years old – by seeing them as adversaries and forcefully fighting them off. Back then, I saw life as an almost constant contest between me and my multitude of enemies, from sickness to storms to darkness to countless possible catastrophes, and it seems I'm still, at 71, sometimes wrestling with life instead of simply living it. Recently, though, I've been seeing this current problem of mine as maybe more like a river to be floated on than a battle to be fought. Maybe life isn't so much a fight as a friend, a convivial adventure instead of an endless struggle. The best way to work with a river is probably to tell it to go where it will and you'll follow, and perhaps I need to say something similar: "Proceed, problem. Take me to a truth I haven't seen before. Let's see what we can do together." When I was 12 (and 30 and 60), I attacked my problems, and almost always lost. Maybe I'm finally finding a new way.

⊨⊬ ⊬⊨

## GROWING DOWN

My grandchildren are "growing up", as the saying goes, but at the same time, their Grandpa Hammy is growing down – and grateful to finally be doing it. Instead of reaching for higher achievements and superior status (which I spent decades doing), I'm walking down into the sweet valley of simple satisfaction. Instead of climbing toward ever more knowledge, I'm resting with the easy wisdom that comes with contentment. Instead of higher and better awards and rewards, I'm searching for the commonplace prizes presented by every present moment. The sight of a small toad hopping down in the grass this morning means way more to me than reaching some lofty goal or accomplishing some tricky task. Let kids be the ones who grow up; this elder citizen is growing down into the fields of cheerful fulfillment.

⊨⊬ ⊬⊨

## A SENSE OF THE INFINITE

I sometimes find myself thinking about elements of life that seem to be infinite – elements that don't have starting points or ending places, that have no boundaries or borders or edges or limits. These are the intangible parts of life, the parts that can't be seen or touched but that stay with us forever and flow without end from everywhere to everywhere. The love we feel for family and friends, for instance, and for life itself, is as infinite as the universe. It has no limits, no boundaries where suddenly the love is blocked and stops. The sky, perhaps, has a far distant place where stars can't shine, but love knows no such place, and will shine unfailingly everywhere and forever. Gentleness, too, is infinite. What barrier can bring gentleness to a stop, or what power can prevail over its soft, unceasing authority? And of course there's the endless present moment, the moment that never starts and never ends and can never be destroyed. The present is infinite, always here and now, always able to endure beyond the borders of space and time in this infinitely vast life we're all living.

⊷⊶

## HEARING THE CALL

In the summer, when I hear birds calling back and forth across the yard, I sometimes make believe they're calling me. "Hello, Ham," I hear them saying, "pay attention to what's happening. Don't miss this amazing day." There are other calls that seem to come to me: the call of the flag in front of our house as it waves in the wind and wants me to watch it carefully; the call of the clock in our living room as it ticks and tells me to make the most of all my moments; the call of a clementine on the counter to come and enjoy its juiciness. As a young boy, I was encouraged to listen for the call to the ministry from a God who seemed to reside somewhere in the sky, but since then I've found another God, the One that lives in all of us, including birds and flags and clocks and clementines, the One that loves to let us know about the beauty of each newborn moment, the One that calls to us to see the sacredness of things. Those are the calls I'm listening for these days.

⊷⊶

## A SLEEK DAY

We bought a new car yesterday – a 2014 Toyota Camry – and its sleek, silvery look made the day feel especially smooth. Partly because the car seemed to shine more than most as we drove it home, the whole afternoon appeared to proceed in a streamlined way. Minutes gracefully came and went, and the sprinkling rain had a stylish look across the town. At home, our late-season lawn seemed especially glossy, and the almost bare tree limbs somehow looked silky. I think we both felt more sophisticated, more stylish, now that we had something so suave sitting in our driveway.

⚒

## A SWEET-TEMPERED AFTERNOON

Today, as I was watching some birds bringing seeds back and forth from the feeder to a bush close by, I happened to also read these words from a poem by Tennyson: "To watch the long bright river drawing slowly / His waters from the purple hill." We live a block away from the Mystic River, and it was almost as if I could see the river at that moment, making its easy way out to the sea on this soft and sleepy afternoon. I saw the birds brightening their day with sunflower seeds, and I saw in my mind the sweet-tempered river "drawing slowly [its] waters from the purple hill[s]" of Mystic and from the measureless sea close by.

⚒

## RESTING

I was resting my elbows on the arm of our sofa just moments ago, and it made me think about how many other things are available to help me loosen up and relax a little. The chairs set around our house, for instance, are simply places for pausing for rest. When I'm sitting in a comfortable chair, it's like the chair is saying, *Stay with me and rest awhile.* Even our carpeted floors are places for easing up and slowing down – soft foot-beds, you might say, where worn-out feet can find some useful rest. I guess, honestly, resting places are presented to me almost everywhere – the sidewalks that are more restful for my feet than the often rutted roads, the cushioned seat in our car that cares for me while I drive, and even, I suppose, the whole earth that's been holding me pleasantly and faithfully up for 73 years. I never have to search to find a place to pause and rest, for the earth is always there.

⇥ ⇤

## A TALE QUICKLY TOLD

It surprises me that I still sometimes consider my personal life so all-important, as though I'm at the center of the universe's show, when the truth is that my life is as brief as a passing shadow, as fleeting as a tale quickly told. In the immeasurable history of the universe, my life span is no more than a snap of the fingers, something that flashes and disappears in a small part of a second. It's a bubble in the stream of time that bursts almost before the everlasting stars have seen it. This doesn't mean my life is insignificant – just that it's not at the center of things, not the axis around which the world revolves. Hamilton Salsich is a wave in the ceaseless river of the universe - a wave that's special, yes, but no more so than the smallest mouse or the breeze that's blowing past our house just now. I love my life, but I hope I can love it no more than I love other people's lives, or the rolling river near our house, or the small birds that bring their beautiful lives to our feeders. It's a little tale, this life of mine, a tale among countless other short and special tales the universe has been telling forever.

⇥ ⇤

## HUMMING MACHINES

Often, while I was waiting for my evening college class to begin, I sat in a lobby at the college surrounded by humming snack machines, and it occasionally got me thinking about the humming minds of students and their teachers. For three hours on fifteen nights each semester, my students and I met together in a small room, and, though each of us was sometimes silent, our minds were always making the steady sounds of earnest thinking. That's what minds do: they silently hum like hardworking snack machines, making endless refreshments, you might say, for our thought-hungry lives. After all, we live on thoughts, all of us. Our thoughts feed us, fill us with spirit and vision, and free us to find new ways to widen our lives. Whether we're working on an important project or just enjoying an idle afternoon, our minds are manufacturing thoughts that can carry us a thousand miles in a millisecond. Our minds are mechanisms made of a wild kind of wisdom, and they hum with the liveliness of limitless snack machines. I tried to keep this in mind as I made my way with my students through our evening classes. In the deadest, most soundless moments of a class, our always animated minds were beating the drums of thoughts and throwing thinking parties inside us. Silence and dullness on the outside, perhaps, but inside, always the purr and pulsation of spirited thoughts.

⇒⊢ ⊣⇐

## A TOE-TAPPING DAY

This morning I was watching our flag in front of the house furling and unfurling in a light wind, and it looked to me like it was somehow keeping time, somehow staying with a certain rhythm in its movements. Then I noticed snowmelt dripping from the roof, drop by drop, in a sort of pleasing cadence, almost in a finger-snapping way. Then I heard an announcer on the radio speaking about some upcoming music, and his words, I noticed, moved in a rhythmical way. Then the music started, a Mozart symphony, and there was a swing in the sounds. As I listened, I kept watching the flag flowing to its own beat and the melting snow dripping from the roof in a steady tempo. It was definitely a rhythmic few moments for me. I was on a planet that was gracefully spinning through space, my heart was keeping a pleasant pace, and several cars passed the house as smoothly as Mozart's music on this toe-tapping day in Mystic.

# FREE-OF-CHARGE

Several years ago, I tried my best to help a friend who was feeling unloved by someone whom he dearly loved, and I recall that a reassuring thought about his situation came to me, one which I shared with him. It occurred to me that my friend was thinking of love as something private and personal. He seemed to be thinking of love as a commodity, a material substance, like money, for instance, something private that could be given from one person to another, something he could then personally own and keep and treasure. His friend had given him her love, much like you might give a special gift, and now she had taken it back, and he felt forsaken and lacking in love. What I realized, and what I shared with him, is that *love is not private or personal*. It sounds crazy, but it struck me as an undeniable fact: love is totally impersonal, simply because it isn't made by any one person, doesn't belong to any one person, and can't be owned by any one person. It's not a material "thing" that can be constructed, given, and then taken away. An analogy that came to me is the air, which is everywhere and is freely available to everyone, just like love. No one would think of saying to someone, "I own this air I'm breathing, and no one can take it away." The air can't be privately owned, and thus can't be given and then recalled, and nether can love. Both air and love are just there – always, and for everyone. While my friend was feeling unloved, all around him love was being breathed in, enjoyed, and then expressed – by his friends, by his family members, by his estranged loved one, by her family, by millions of strangers, and, of course, by him. My friend, like all of us, was absolutely surrounded by love, but he, like many of us, couldn't see it and feel it, because he wanted it to be private, his own, something he could stow away and stockpile. As with many of us, he wanted the love to be for him personally. He wanted to own love and keep love, and he felt like his loved one took it away from him. The truth is, though – and this is what I shared with him – that *no one can take away any of the love that always surrounds us and is part of us.* Love is wider and wilder and bigger and more boundless than any one person. It's with us always, like the endless air. When we're despondent and desperate, the air is still there, waiting for us to breathe it in, and so is love. The love may not be specifically and personally directed toward us, including my friend, but that's just because it's too immense, too never-ending. My friend's loved one had turned away from him, but the love that she and all of us are part of was still with him. *He couldn't possibly escape from it,* just as he can't escape from air. The years have passed, but I still hope my friend, come what may, can always breathe in the undying power of free-of-charge, freewheeling, and limitless love.

<hr/>

## A TOGETHERNESS CONCERT
Last night, we attended a dance concert at Connecticut College, and it was a truly astonishing performance by gifted young dancers. It's amazing to me that students taking a dance class three

hours per week were able to present such a fluid and refined performance. I couldn't help but think of the idea of "togetherness" as I watched these inventive dancers glide around the stage. There was cohesion in their movements, a kind of easy harmony among their bodies as they smoothly set forth the themes of the various dances. There was an inspiring singleness among the dancers, as though they were one blended dancer instead of many. There was cohesiveness among them, and camaraderie, and the close bonds that bring people together to make something special. Our admiration and thanks go to the young dancers and the college's Dance Department for doing what the whole world needs to do: work as one in fellowship and concord.

---

## SUNS IN DEWDROPS

I recall seeing, on many summer mornings, the sunlight reflected in small drops of dew in the grass, and, as I think about it on this gray day in winter, it seems as though the sun itself was in those summer dewdrops. When I stand in front of a mirror, I am, in a sense, in the reflection, since it looks exactly like me, and so perhaps it could be said that the sun is, in a way, inside each drop of summer dew. When I walk across a summer lawn, perhaps I walk among millions of sparkling suns. On this winter day, when grayness gives its quiet gifts to us, it's good to remember being among dewdrops with suns inside them.

---

## A WATERED GARDEN

As I look forward to seeing Cia watering her flowers this spring and summer, it makes sense to think of my own life as a lucky and well-watered garden. After all, whether I always notice it or not, things are continuously growing in my life – fresh thoughts, feelings I've never felt before, new cells arising inside me, youthful breath for my lungs each moment. Each moment, in fact, provides a brand-new start for me, like a young shoot bursting through the soil in springtime. Even on my dullest days, promise and opportunity is popping into bloom inside me and all around me. The garden of this good world is fertile and fruitful. I just need to open my eyes and see it.

⊷⊶

## A WELL OF WATER

It's amazing to me how many "wells of water" I fail to notice – I mean, how many outpourings of thoughtfulness I sometimes overlook as I pursue my personal agendas. Cia and I are given the gift of good water from our backyard well, but I'm also given another kind of gift again and again, the gift of friendliness – and I don't always notice or appreciate it. Just yesterday, I spoke to a man on the phone about some confusing issues concerning insurance, and, as I think back on it, he offered his helpfulness in an altogether generous way. He good-naturedly gave me the gift of his expertise, stopping several times to make sure I understood. As we were finishing our conversation, he even offered to come to our house for a conference to further explain things. This man was an ungrudging giver, a spilling-over source of advice and reassurance – but did I hang up and praise his work to my wife? Nope – just checked off another job on the agenda. This morning, though, as I was washing the breakfast dishes and watching the water flow from the faucet with abundance, I thought again of this man's gracious goodwill yesterday, and I smiled in thankfulness.

⊷⊶

## DOES A BREEZE EVER HAVE A PROBLEM?

Sometimes, when some problem seems to be standing in my way, it helps me if breezes are blowing outside. Then, I either sit by a window and watch the breezes swaying the trees, or, better still, I walk outside, and soon a question comes to me: Does a breeze ever have a problem? A breeze blows freely and flexibly, flowing easily around trees and homes and cars and hills. If a breeze bumps up against an obstacle – what I might call a "problem" – it simply slides around or over or under it and continues on its easy way. You might say that any situation a breeze finds itself in is tailor-made for it, because it will always perform with style and effortlessness, and soon press on with its graceful voyage across the land. I guess the ease and smoothness of breezes brings home their best lessons to me. "Just loosen up, Ham", they seem to say. "Be like a breeze. Go around, over, or under, and the problems will suddenly be transformed into opportunities for elegance and artistry."

## ABANDONING

The word "abandon" often carries a negative connotation, but I occasionally find myself living with a positive and useful kind of "abandon". As a noun, the word can mean living with a lack of inhibition or restraint, and every so often I feel myself sort of sailing loose from my moorings and turning a few moments or hours into an impetuous escapade. I'm usually a fairly logical and predictable person, but now and then I like to live like a sailor with good sails, supportive winds, and no schedule. Even a few minutes of living with abandon – perhaps singing old songs as I ride my bike, or mixing mints and grapes with my scrambled eggs, or skipping with my grandchildren – can balance the seriousness of life with some wholesome whimsy and gladness.

# NEW SIGNS, NEW EVERYTHING

As we drove along the interstate this morning, there were signs I'd never seen before. These signs, naming exits and streets and towns, had actually been there for years, but in a sense, they were as new this morning as the sunlight shining on them. After all, since yesterday, new dust had settled on them in brand new patterns, the weather had reworked them by further wearing them down, and the light was landing on them in ever so slightly new ways. In that sense, these were signs I'd never seen before, signs that seemed newly redecorated, rejuvenated, and I might say *re-made* in the hours and moments before we passed them. The signs seemed to almost flash their newness at us as we passed. I realized, later, that this implies a startling fact about our Universe – namely, the newness *of all things*. Despite my usual inability to notice it, there is newness everywhere – in signs on the interstate, in clouds assembling in the sky in ways no one has seen before, in cars covered with salt in patterns that are each, in tiny ways, different from any previous pattern in the history of cars and salt. I couldn't stop thinking about it as the day passed – this newness, this freshness, this utter novelty and originality of everything. It seemed like an astonishing life I was living, a life where starting fresh happens every second, a life in which all things – including me – are no more than one second old!

═╬ ╬═

## ABDICATING

According to one dictionary, to "abdicate" means to give up being a queen or king, and I would actually love do that -- would love to stop pretending to be the king of my life. In fact, I wonder if the best way to live is to let life itself be the king instead of little me. Life, in all its vastness and mystery and supremacy, surely knows more about what's best for me than I do. Me trying to be the king of every second of every day is like one wave trying to preside over the whole ocean, or a single star trying to rule the endless universe. Each moment of my life is fashioned from an immeasurable number of sources and causes, and it seems bizarre to me that I sometimes think I can control all these forces, waving my scepter like a hopeful but clueless king. I indulge in this silly charade every day, but occasionally I decide to set my make-believe crown aside and let the only real ruler, the everlasting Universe -- some call it God, some Allah, some simply Now -- hold sway. It's astonishing what this remarkable Queen-King can do.

═╬ ╬═

## ABOUNDING

"Abound" is a word that isn't often used in writings and conversations these days, but this morning it seemed surprisingly suitable. From our sunroom, where Cia and I were having breakfast, I could see a sky abounding in blueness, seemingly overflowing with the color's various shades. The trees around the house abounded in bright sunlight, seeming almost crowded with light, as though the sunshine was packing the trees as fully as possible. And I might add that Cia and I, as we enjoyed our omelets and coffee, were abounding in feelings of good fortune. You might say our life these days abounds with satisfaction. The hours seem stuffed with fulfillment. Like all of us, we do sometimes face difficulties, but they are usually neutralized by the sustaining quietness that crowds our days and nights.

⚏

## BEING FREE

There are times when I see, with surprising ease, that I've been given the gift of complete freedom. On those occasions, it becomes clear to me that, rather than being bound within a separate, isolated, vulnerable body, I am actually an essential part of a boundless and harmonious universe. Atoms that make up the mind and body I call mine were shaped at the same moment that stars started to shine and the earth to spin, and thus have sailed freely through countless eons. My thoughts, too, have flown to me on the freest wings, sailing into my life in casual, relaxed ways from who knows where, and I can take those thoughts beyond all boundaries, wherever I please. Most of the time, I confess, I do feel bound up by all kinds of limits, but at certain special times I know I'm as free as winds that flow from wherever to anywhere.

⚏

## ABOVE

These days, I find myself increasingly thankful for the many things that are above me. Trees, for instance, seem like older sisters and brothers standing above me as I type this in the backyard. The sky spreads its ever-present and reassuring sheet above me, and above the sky, I know the concealed stars are shining their trustworthy lights. I think, too, of the countless people whom I consider to be, in some sense, above me – those who slowly store up wisdom and then share it with others, those who use bravery to beat down hopelessness, and those who love like it's all they should ever be doing. When I say they're above me, I don't mean to disparage myself, but simply to say how much I look up to those who seem so strong in their goodness that no hostile force can defeat them. I look up to them because they do seem, in a way, above me, like sunshine is above the summer grass and the steadfast stars are above us all.

⸺✦⸺

## CAPRICIOUS LEAVES AND THOUGHTS

In the autumn, I sometimes watch leaves seemingly idling in the air as they lower themselves slowly down to the ground, and it occasionally brings to mind the way my mind sometimes seems to linger and glide and wander with any winds of thoughts that waft through it. It usually annoys me to see this kind of capriciousness in my thinking, but it's pleasing to see the little autumn leaves straying aimlessly around and finally settling haphazardly on the grass. The leaves take lazy routes as they fall, and my mind, too, occasionally sidles around and around as it works its way through some issue. I wonder: Why should the whimsicality and waywardness of my mind be any less enjoyable to watch than the falling leaves I see sailing casually among autumn trees?

⸺✦⸺

## ALL SET

It's reassuring to realize, each morning, that a thousand things are ready to assist me during the day, and that they were made ready with absolutely no assistance from me. I sometimes smugly think of myself as my own source and supplier of the tools of success, but it's simply not the case -- not when I consider, for instance, my car that is occasionally cared for by master mechanics, with no help from me; the streets that have been kept smooth and clean for my car, with no help from me; the stoplights that successfully send me and others from one intersection to another, with no help from me; the sunshine that makes it easy to see the promising spring trees, with no help from me; and the trees themselves that are making major miracles on these mild April days, with no help from me. I'm set to have a fine day each morning, mostly because of the countless tasks undertaken by people and forces unfamiliar and far away, the loyal laborers who do their duties so that ease and comfort can be a much bigger part of my life than pressure and stress.

⚊⊰⊹⊱⚊

## AN ULTRA-UNION

Cia and I are in St. Louis for a Salsich family reunion, but it seems to me that the prefix is not the proper one. Instead of a reunion, perhaps we should see it as something like an ultra-union. The prefix "re" implies that we're joining in a union *again*, as though an earlier union was broken and now we are redoing it, but the truth is that our family union has never been broken, and in fact cannot be broken. Actually, all of us on earth – people, plants, animals, even the widespread sky and mountains and oceans – are part of an enduring union, a family of wonders working together without realizing it. We are all as closely connected as the air we share and the sunlight that lands on each of us. There's the family of the Salsichs, yes, but then there's what we might call the family of the universe, which consists of all the miracles ever made – every person, speck of dust, maple tree, and mouse. It's a family - a union - that cannot come to an end, cannot be de-unioned, and therefore never needs to be re-unioned. We are enjoying our gathering in St. Louis, but we're thinking of it not so much as a reunion, but more as an ultra-union – a celebration to heighten and intensify our appreciation of the everlasting union of which all of us across the universe have always been members.

⟫⟪

## BEAUTIFUL NOISE

I've often been bothered by the "noise" that seems to inevitably be present in doctors' and dentists' waiting rooms – the constant sounds of television shows or recorded music – but something happened one morning that made me rethink my attitude toward it. As I was walking outside in the yard, I noticed that I was accompanied by the sounds of strong winds and cars on the distant interstate. The sounds were steady and insistent, and wherever I walked in the yard, they were always there. I couldn't escape them, just as I can't escape the televised or musical sounds in the waiting rooms. The difference was that I *took pleasure* in the sounds in the yard. Instead of struggling against them, instead of classifying them as "noise" and wishing they would stop, I listened to them with acceptance and appreciation. The sounds of the winds and cars weren't what I would call "beautiful", but they were somehow interesting and worthy of note. Perhaps, on my future visits to dentists' or doctors' offices, I will try to come with ears that are less closed and resistant, and more relaxed and approving – ears that welcome and appreciate rather than resist and shut down.

⟫⟪

# ALWAYS AMAZED

I sometimes feel like I'm in a befuddling maze, which is why, perhaps, I often feel *a-mazed* by everything around me. Like many of us, I enjoy pretending that my life is laid out in well-marked roads, and that I know exactly where I'm going and how to get there, but the truth is that I've been in an almost daily maze since November of 1941. Honestly, I still have little or no idea who I am or why things happen or where I should be going, and it is in this sense that I feel almost constantly amazed, as though I've been endlessly wandering in a maze for 72 years. Perhaps, though, I should say "labyrinth" instead of maze, for in a labyrinth there is no worry of being lost, since all paths in due course lead to the center and back out. A labyrinth is a light-hearted place to be, since all choices are somehow the right ones, and seeming mistakes end up showing you the way. I guess life, for me, has been like a puzzling but relaxing labyrinth. It's like a maze made for my pleasure and instruction, a place where patience can turn mistakes into miracles.

## MOONS AND PARAGRAPHS

An almost full moon is shining through the trees as I type this – as I take my time to try to make a full and finished paragraph – and its light looks like it might be good luck for my writing. It's a complete moon, and I want to make a complete piece of writing. I want to place words in a suitable order so there's an unbroken series of ideas doing their work side by side - in partnership, in unison, as one. The moon in this pre-dawn darkness makes a circle of light, and perhaps my paragraph can produce a circle of thoughts – a circle that might, in its own way, shine with the fullness and simplicity of the moon. I think of other things that are full – this earth full of force and promise, the sea full of hopeful life – and I hope my small assortment of phrases and sentences may be full of its own kind of influential life. Even if I am the only person who will read my paragraph, perhaps it will shine as I say the words silently, shine like something in good shape and strong, the unbroken and undamaged thoughts of one man on a very early moonlit morning.

## ALWAYS DANCING

Delycia has been encouraging me to take dancing lessons with her, and I'm leaning toward saying yes, but actually, we're always dancing already. Just walking around the house, just moving our legs in a free-flowing way, is a kind of dancing. A person confined to a wheelchair would marvel at the fluid movements of our bodies as we walk from room to room. To a paralyzed person, our effortless walking would be a miraculous dance. In fact, our bodies are always dancing in other innumerable ways. Blood is streaming through us with a smoothness that dancers would envy, and all our cells are doing their innumerable duties with a proper pace and style. Our lungs, too, are lifting and falling with the poise of dancers, and of course, our hearts keep a measured beat as they bring us gracefully around the "dance floor" of each day. Yes, Delycia and I are *always* dancing, so perhaps she's right. Perhaps we should take some lessons to learn how to take our already classy dancing to the next level.

＝+ +＝

## BACKYARD CHURCH

In warm weather, we often worship in our beautiful backyard "church". The door to our church is the back door of our house, which opens into a sanctuary of blessed sights and sounds. There are no stained-glass windows, but the sunlight on the leaves and limbs of the trees lends a consecrated look to our place of worship. The floor is just our old, good grass, and the pews are the lawn chairs that let us relax while we worship. Of course, we can also worship by wandering through Delycia's hallowed flower gardens, or by simply standing still and listening to the choirs of birds and feeling the flow of the always ceremonious breezes. We worship no god who stays up in the sky, no deity who decrees that some will suffer in hell. In our backyard church, we honor the sacredness that is all good and resides in all things – in shaking leaves, in tulips turning in a puff of wind, even in the old stones that set the gardens apart. Our minister is sometimes a squirrel, sometimes simply the vast, sociable sky.

＝+ +＝

## ALWAYS GOING SOMEWHERE

In my busy teenage years, I recall my mother often saying that I was "always going somewhere", and, in a strange way, I still am. Actually, I have no choice, since everything in this universe is constantly stirring or shifting or racing. There is no such thing as standing still. Even when I'm sitting in my laziest way, all my cells are transforming in a swift and unceasing manner. The electrons in the hydrogen atoms that compose a sizeable part of my body are traveling fast enough, physicists say, to circle the earth in 18 seconds, and the planet I'm spending my life on is soaring around the sun at something like 67,000 miles per hour. Plus, even while I'm doing my morning meditation in silence and stillness, the solar system I belong to is barreling around the Milky Way at close to 600,000 miles per hour. So yes, mom, I'm still always going somewhere in this astonishing life you gave me.

⊷⊱ ⊰⊶

## APPLAUSE FOR GREAT AND SMALL THINGS
### (after seeing *Richard II* with Delycia at Shakespeare and Company, Lenox, MA)

I wonder why I don't applaud more often for the great and small things in life – the large and little miracles that make up almost every moment of my days. I let so many marvels slip by me with barely a notice, and no applause. I don't mean I should be constantly clapping my hands, but surely I could send out at least silent praises more frequently for the gifts I get from the world. I'm thinking of this today because yesterday Delycia and I saw a riveting performance of *Richard II*, at the end of which the applause was strangely faint and fleeting. Within a few seconds, the clapping stopped and the audience started for the exits. This amazed me, but perhaps it shouldn't have, for I sometimes show a similar lack of appreciation for special performances. This morning, for instance, the fountain beside the pool at the hotel where we're staying is flowing beautifully, doing a small, lovely performance, but I've hardly noticed it. A brightly colored beach ball is floating along the surface of the pool in silent rolls and turns, and the songs of two birds are sailing from two trees, but I've been too busy to listen. They're small, unnoticed miracles in my life that's overflowing with them, like the theater yesterday that spilled over with the wisdom and elegance of Shakespeare done perfectly, but was almost empty of applause.

⊷ ⊶

## CAN'T WAIT TO SEE

Years ago, a woman I knew experienced some serious suffering, and I remember being astonished to hear her say, in the very midst of her misery, "I can't wait to see how this is going to transform into something good for me." She was smiling as she said it, not a wide, showy smile, but a modest one that simply said, "I see something good in all this." There was a sense of self-assurance, almost a sanguine buoyancy in her smile, as though she understood that goodness sometimes leaves its best gifts in the center of suffering. She was almost excited, it seemed, to see how peace and wisdom would somehow work their wizardry inside her suffering – somehow transform her anguish into understanding and expansion. I think of her sometimes when I'm working through some small misfortune. I see her smile in her wise way. I hear her say, "A gift is being given to you. Don't miss it."

⊷ ⊶

## APPLES AND THANKS

"My heart is like an apple-tree
Whose boughs are bent with thick-set fruit."

-- Christina Rossetti, "A Birthday"

On autumn days, I often think of apples, since they are moist and bright by the millions on branches all over New England, and I also think of those of us who feel lucky to be loaded with the gifts received in a long life. Apple trees give us apples in the fall, and some of us feel fortunate to be able to give back to others some of the gifts life has given us in our 65+ serendipitous years. I've survived into my 70s because countless numbers of people prepared my way and then worked beside me to make sure I stayed on course. The gifts I've been given, like our East Coast apples, are far too many to be counted, but they don't have to be counted, just given back with gratitude. Trees give apples; I give thanks.

# ADMIRING RADIANCE

(written on the winter solstice)

As is fitting in this special season of darkness and light, we sometimes have candles shining around the house after dinner, sending out their soft light as we read or write by the fire. Every so often, I pause and simply admire the radiance of the candles. They don't take up much space on the tables, but they spread a large and friendly light through the rooms. They make me think of other kinds of helpful light – the light of lamps that allow people to see and appreciate each other; the headlights of cars that show us the roads to our destinations; the silent light of stars above our sometimes anxious world; and – best of all – the light of thoughts that continually flash and show us the way we should go. On this evening of the darkest day of the year, as Delycia and I drove home from a performance of "A Christmas Carol" in Hartford, I loved seeing the lights along the way – the comforting lamps in windows of homes, the sparkling Christmas lights in yards, and the shining streetlights that somehow gave a certain splendor to the darkness. I found myself thinking, for some reason, of the great light of the sun – the source of all our light – and the even greater light of vast, never-ending forces like love and gentleness. I seemed to see and feel the light that shines in all places, all hearts, and all times.

⊶ ⊷

## BACK TO BOYHOOD

I occasionally listen to old time radio shows on the Internet, and they always take me happily back to my boyhood in the less worrisome times of the 40's and 50's. As I listen to "The Challenge of the Yukon", starring Sergeant Preston and his loyal husky, King, I'm carried back to 1517 Holly Drive, the pleasant house where we stretched out on the floor each night to listen to our favorite shows. Hearing again the kindly voice of Mr. Keen, tracer of lost persons, brings back warm memories of times when things seemed less wearing – days when an unsophisticated fifteen-minute radio show left you ready for another eight hours of easy sleep.

⊶ ⊷

## BEING UNIVERSE-CENTERED

I guess I'm no more self-centered than most of us, but from now on, I'm looking to let something else become the center of my life, and I've chosen the entire universe. I want to become more universe-centered. Instead of pondering the problems my little self seems to always have, I'd like to wonder more about what's happening outside of "me" – what's happening in the homes of people who are suffering with illness or scarcity, and in the homes of people who feel lucky to be alive; what's happening in the forests and valleys across the world, where animals and plants prosper while I fret over my paltry problems; what's happening, even, among the planets and stars as they swirl me along on our endless passage

33

through time without end. I grow weary of worrying about this small segment of the universe called "Hamilton Salsich". There are majestic miracles surrounding me, for millions of miles on all sides, and I want to stay centered there. I want to set my "self" off to the side and see, almost for the first time, the wondrous universe that's been waiting for me.

⇒+ +⇐

## SONGS WHILE I'M SLEEPING

I awoke several times last night and listened for a few minutes to the singing of the insects outside, and it has me thinking, this morning, about some of the other things that happen while I'm sleeping. For the few hours that I'm asleep, the universe, as always, is a stirring place. Besides the music of countless crickets and katydids, there must be limitless kinds of activities among nighttime animals as they live their important lives – the rushing and shoving and soaring that's essential for the creatures that carry on with their lives while I'm lying among soft sheets. There's the nighttime work of people who prepare essential things for the rest of us while we sleep – the third-shift factory workers who make the beds that we sleep on, the grocery employees who get food up on the shelves so we can select what we need in the morning, the employees of power companies who keep our nightlights lit. While I'm sleeping, airplanes are streaking across countries and seas on essential missions, hospitals are helping people prepare for better lives, and police officers in cities and towns are taking their peacekeeping work seriously. While I'm fortunate to be finding a few hours of rest beside my wife, rivers are flowing as fast as they always are, and the steadfast stars are doing their shining, as always, above us.

⇒+ +⇐

## BIRTHDAY IMMATURITY

Many years ago I was surprised to find that the basic definition for the word "immature" is "not fully developed" -- in other words, still growing -- and ever since, I have hoped that I will remain immature until the moment of my death. Thinking about this, I proudly recall a recent birthday that I celebrated in a totally immature way. Since I am still growing in my 70s – still changing, still advancing, still learning – it seems fitting that I behaved in a completely boyish manner. What was wonderful was that I was with one of my favorite boys, my grandson Josh, which made it easy to have fun in a thoroughly unsophisticated and childish way. I was also with Delycia, who's more spry and sprightly than many teens I've known, and so the three of us formed a team of totally foolish friends. We were at a carnival-type cafe for pizza and game-playing, and we played our hearts out. We raced cars, boats, and planes; we threw small balls and basketballs; we even shot and killed monsters of all sorts. (Delycia was our best shooter, by far.) We raced from game to game like the silliest of kids. We were giddy and scatterbrained, but oh so happy. Delycia and I were in the springtime of our lives, a couple of immature, retired teenagers taking pleasure in being young with a boy who does it beautifully.

⊨⊹ ⊹⊨

## WANDERING THOUGHTS

"… those thoughts that wander through eternity."

-- John Milton, "Paradise Lost"

These days, when I recall my elementary school teachers saying that I had a "wandering mind", I actually feel grateful for that unfettered, rambling way of thinking. Although it's sometimes fun to *pretend* that I carefully manufacture my own thoughts, the truth is that they cascade into my mind -- mostly through reading and conversation -- in a totally undisciplined and impersonal manner. It's as if, in Milton's words, zillions of thoughts "wander through eternity", and some of them happen to spill into me as I'm doing my own kind of wandering. What's appealing to me about this is that the thoughts I think have previously spilled into countless other minds before they reach mine, and thus they bring along to me the immeasurable treasures of countless thinkers over the centuries. I no more make my own thoughts than a river makes its own water. Rivers flow because a limitless number of rills, runnels, and streams flow into them, and I entertain thoughts because innumerable other thinkers have welcomed these ambling, dawdling thoughts that forever "wander through eternity" and fall, for a few moments or hours, into my small, strolling-around life.

# BLUE SKYING

Not long ago, when Delycia was sharing some suggestions about placement of our new patio furniture, she said I shouldn't take her too seriously, because she was just "blue skying". When I asked her to explain, she said when there's a blue sky, she likes to think that airplane pilots feel more free to follow their whims and wander wherever they wish, just like she was letting her thoughts do. When you "blue sky", she said, you sort of think – and live – without laws, at least for a while. As I've thought about it since then, it seems a good way to live – to sometimes let your life lift off the runway and be on the loose, like a plane in a sunny sky. Thoughts, especially, should be sometimes set free to veer and swerve and stray in this direction or that, as Delycia was doing so delightfully. In a way, life brings "blue skies" to me constantly, if only I could notice. Most of the limitations I live by are built by my own beliefs, and once I see this, the sky of my life can clear and I can chart my own course. In a sky or life that's blue, the clouds are gone and I can dare to be brave, both with ideas for furniture and directions for my life.

## TAKING MYSELF LIGHTLY

When I recall hearing someone say that angels can fly because they take themselves lightly, it always sounds like excellent advice for me. I'm not interested in flying, but I would like to shed some of the seriousness which weighs me down. I sometimes walk around like I have loads of responsibilities on my shoulders – like I'm some special superman who has serious tasks to perform, tasks that simply must be done by me alone. On those days, I take myself way too seriously. Unlike angels, I'm weighed down by a dreamed-up sense of my own importance. On those days, flying is out and self-absorbed slogging is in. On other days, lucky for me, I get loose from this seriousness and see myself for what I am – just a small twirl in the everlasting dance of a bighearted universe. My silly self-importance disappears like a small star in the vastness of dawn. I feel light on those days – light and free and ready to relax with life instead of wrestle with it.

⊨⊩

## A HAND OF WELCOME

The word "acquiescence" often carries a negative connotation – a sense that a person is reluctantly giving in – but it's interesting that the word derives from the Latin for "quiet", which offers a fresh perspective on it. When I acquiesce to whatever's happening in my life, perhaps I've simply settled into a disposition of relaxed acceptance. Perhaps the word implies embracing even the worst situations with calmness and a kind of respectfulness, and then studying them and trying to learn from them. Rather than necessarily suggesting a submissive attitude, acquiescence may actually stem from understanding that saying "yes" to the universe's plans for me can prepare the way for a wider kind of wisdom. I may not always *love* what's happening in my life, but bowing to it can bring the inner quietness and light that learning something new often produces. I might even drop the 'a' in the word. Perhaps I want to keep the *quiescent* kind of life I seem to have fallen into, a life marked, not by the sluggishness that sometimes shows up in retirement, but by a powerful kind of peacefulness, which often can come from just accepting what's happening. I guess I'm slowly learning to extend a welcome to problems instead of opposing them, partly because acceptance is simply more restful than resistance, but also because working *with* a problem instead of against it seems to make my old life, in little and large ways, more triumphant day by day. Back in my youthful 50's, I was often stressed and frenzied from fighting with problems, but now, in my fairly hassle-free 70's, I'm trying to put out a hand of welcome to trouble, just to see what possibilities it might present.

⇥ ⇤

## THANKS

When I discovered this morning that the history of the word "thank" connects it, in a circuitous way, to the word "think", it made sense to me, since simply thinking carefully about my life always makes me feel thankful. Only a totally unthinking person would fail to praise the beautiful things that brighten all my days. Just the fact that I am somehow here, right now, on this startling planet, and living this always surprising life, is grounds for the sincerest gratitude. Who gave me this gift of a vast and silver sky above me and ten fingers to type words on a laptop that win my heart when I read them? How did it happen that the "big bang" so many billions of years ago eventually, in November of 1941, presented the universe with a baby boy named Hamilton, who has now seen so many miracles it makes his 74-year-old head spin? Just thinking about my marvelous life makes me want to wave and dance, but since I'm presently riding in a car beside my beautiful driver, Delycia, I'll just say a quiet "Thanks to one and all!", and throw her an appreciative kiss as we sail down the interstate.

---

## BUZZ

There's always enthusiasm in the air around our riverside house in the first days of springtime weather. Delycia and I watch the birds winging their way across our yard from tree to tree, and it always seems to get us going with greater eagerness on our seasonal chores. While she works with attentiveness among her steadily blossoming flowers, I sweep and dust the house with unusual zeal. In this early promising weather, I seem to care about keeping the house as clean as she always does, and I do my jobs as though they were joyous tasks I can't help but take pleasure in. While she sits on her beloved soil and sets in bulbs and shoots, I might shine up bookshelves and wash the shower walls. While she wheels a wheelbarrow full of flowers around the yard, I might find satisfaction in seeing the carpets get even cleaner than they usually are. I stop occasionally to watch the birds going at breakneck speed from tree to tree, and sometimes I see what seems to be dozens of small birds dancing beside a bush. Nearby, Delycia is working with passion to prepare some soil, and close by some squirrels are springing with good spirit along the stones in our wall.

---

## CAN YOU SPREAD OUT THE SKY?

When I do even a small task with success, every so often I secretly salute myself for being so smart, so capable and clever, and it's then that I wish someone would show me the sky around sunset. "Can you spread out the sky like this?" they might say, or "Can you carry ships on your back like the sea?" There's nothing wrong with being happy to have the ability to get a few things done, but when I start slapping myself on the back and beaming with puffed-up self-importance, I need a friend to find me the right path again. I need someone to say, once again, that I am simply a breeze in the boundless wind of the universe, just a small shaft of light in the limitless light of eternity. That doesn't mean I'm not skillful, just no more skillful than the smallest house wren or the sea that supports massive ships. When I start thinking I'm something extra-special, a friend could find me a stone that's been around for billions of years and say, "You've been here how long, Ham – 70-some years? And you think you're extra-special? This stone has survived dinosaurs, the Middle Ages, and millions of mighty storms, and what have you done? Yes, you're special, but so are all stones and blades of grass and drifting winds and lights in sunsets." That would put me in my place – an extraordinary place, for sure, in a universe where all things have been extraordinary right from the start.

⚓ ⚓

## CAPTURING THE PRESENT

Since the word "accept" derives from the Latin word for "capture", I've sometimes thought that I should actually try to capture the present moment instead of simply accepting it. Centuries ago, when you said you wanted to accept something, you might have meant that you wanted to literally capture it – to seize it, snatch it, and take it away with you. I wonder if I could live that way, sort of like a cat sitting beside the hole of a mouse – in this case, the present moment – ready to pounce and take the moment prisoner. And it would have to be *any* moment, not just one that makes me happy. A cat captures any mouse, and perhaps I could set my sight on capturing any and every present moment. Perhaps I could sit beside the hole of the present and prepare to tenderly take prisoner any moment that makes its appearance, be it emaciated or majestic, sinister or inspiring. I could be an alert, good-natured cat – a sweet-hearted feline who simply wants to savor and absorb every single moment. I could quietly capture each moment and consume it with a calm, catlike kind of delight.

⊷✦⊶

## CHANGING MY MIND

I've "changed my mind" millions of times, and lately I've come to see each of those changes as a sort of sunrise inside me. Each change was not just a change of thought, but more like a switch in minds, as if I replaced one mind with another, as if changing my mind brought a whole new world of thoughts to my life. And actually, doesn't each new thought start a fresh flow of other thoughts in our minds? Thoughts can work wonders the way sunrises start new days. A thought is not a material thing we can hold in our hands, but more like a light that illuminates, for a moment, not just our minds but our lives. It's like our minds change into brand new minds when a new thought dawns like daybreak inside us.

⊷✦⊶

## ON NOT JUDGING RIVERS

For most of my 70+ years, I have been a fairly judgmental person – but I'm trying hard to change. I've spent a good part of my waking hours passing judgments on situations, events, and people. I judged every situation as either good or bad, helpful or detrimental; an event either worked to my advantage or didn't; and a person was either right or wrong, nice or not so nice, young or old, smart or not so smart. It's surprising that I didn't thoroughly exhaust myself with all this passionate handing down of verdicts and pronouncements. Actually, some time ago, I decided to stop being a full-time judge – to retire from the judge's "bench", you might say. I was weary from having to constantly appraise everything that came my way, and I decided I wanted to *enjoy* instead of judge. I wanted to sit by – or swim in – the river of life and simply appreciate its surprising movements, without having to continuously give my considered opinions about how well or poorly it was flowing. It's an interesting metaphor, and it brings me around to my privileged role as an English teacher. Over my long and lucky years in the classroom, I took seriously my obligation to judge my students' performances in class, but I always did it with the clear understanding that my judgments were fairly superficial, and, in the big picture, *fairly insignificant.* Judging whether my students could write a shipshape essay or use semicolons with precision was an essential part of my job, but those academic pronouncements of mine said almost nothing about the vast and undiscovered mystery that was each student's life. Those lives flowed past me in the classroom like inscrutable rivers, and what I enjoyed most about teaching was trying to simply appreciate that flow, those irreplaceable adolescent human beings, those matchless creations of the universe. A river changes constantly and sometimes astonishingly, and so did all my many hundreds of students. Every chance I got, I put down my judge's gavel and simply appreciated the remarkable rivers of their lives. Now, in my upcoming retirement, I'm hoping to do the same, more and more, with my still steadily flowing and still surprising life.

⊫+⊨

## ONE STUDENT'S FIRST DAY

On this, the first day of classes at my former school, this freshly retired teacher was a struggling new student at a different kind of school. For far too long this morning, my wife and I worked as hard as I've ever worked at learning something new, and, looking back, it looks like I was strictly a C student. The school was the Westerly YMCA, and the class was called "Silver Sneakers", a name that doesn't come close to suggesting the kind of mystifying exercises I was called upon to carry out. This was a class advertised as a relatively unproblematic approach to conditioning for seniors, but, to me, that's a little like saying hikes in the White Mountains are promenades in the park. From the first minute, I felt like I was 14 again and floundering in a class beyond my skills. As our skilled and spirited teacher called out commands, I stumbled and fumbled and flayed around. When she wanted our feet to move to the right, mine went left; when my hips were supposed to swing in circles, they threw themselves back and forth like total flops as hips. It was like 9th grade math class all over again: I couldn't understand the teacher's directions, everyone but me was making it seem easy, and all I wanted was to stay out of sight in the far back and break free from that room as soon as possible. I was an unsure and confused student, like maybe a few million others in these early weeks of school. My message to other befuddled students: Stay brave. If a furrowed old fellow like me can learn something new, so can you.

⭲⭰

## COMFORTABLE WORDS

". . .when he spake and cheered his Table Round
With [. . .] comfortable words."

-- Alfred, Lord Tennyson, "The Idylls of the King"

In my reading not long ago, I came across Tennyson's phrase "comfortable words", and I wondered if I should pay more attention to those kinds of words in the future. The word "comfort" derives from the Latin word for "strength", suggesting that strong words, those that communicate sincerely and clearly, can also be the most comfortable ones. We say something is comfortable when it's soothing and restful, and perhaps strong, straightforward words, whether written or spoken, can bring some of that kind of comfort to us. After all, sometimes just being in the presence of wholesome strength can cause us to rest in reassurance, knowing that not much can harm us with so much forthright spirit close by. Words that do their work with honesty and force can reassure us, settle us down, and send us toward some faith that this world can be considerably more comfortable than painful.

# PERFECT BALANCE

When I do yoga exercises, I always have a difficult time with the various balancing positions, but the universe itself certainly knows how to keep its balance. If balancing is defined as a state of equilibrium where all forces are perfectly matched by equal opposing forces, then the universe is a master of the art of balancing. There are countless forces at work, but they all seem to offset each other perfectly. There are strong storms, but sunshine is just as strong. There's sadness, but it's always balanced, somewhere, somehow, and soon enough, by happiness. There's sickness, but health enduringly flows onward all around it. There's the sorrow of death everywhere we turn, but life is always there too, flourishing in its invincible way. For every dismal nightfall there's a rousing sunrise. What all this means is that the universe is in perfect equilibrium, flawlessly poised, unassailably steady and stable. There is plenty of discord in the world, but if we look closely, we see that harmony always quickly neutralizes it with its own powerful pull. At the end of the day, all that really exists is perfectly balanced forces cancelling each other out, thereby maintaining the eternal symmetry of things. If the universe were doing yoga exercises with me, it could unquestionably teach me a few things about keeping a strong, steady balance.

———

## PLEASANTLY BORED

These days, the phrase "pleasantly bored" might come close to describing my lifestyle. I don't mean that my life is uninteresting or tedious, but simply that it's not as serious and unsmiling as it has sometimes been. I still find life fairly fascinating, but in a more leisurely way – in a laid-back way that has loosened me up and allowed me to slow down among the activities of my days. True, some of this is because I am retired from full-time work, but some of my softer, gentler approach to daily life stems from seeing more clearly, as the years have passed, that being always focused – the opposite of being bored – can bring about an intensity that soon grows tiresome for friends and family. For me, being intense about something has included being almost *severe* in my attentiveness, and sometimes humorless as well. When I was focused, I was not bored, true, but I was also sometimes not a pleasant person to be around. Nowadays, I am focused in a more amiable and easygoing way. I am focused not so much on the end results of activities, but on the pleasures that come from just *partaking* in the activities. I guess I shrug more than I used to, as when I say to myself, "So you didn't mow the lawn in absolutely straight lines. (shrug) So what? (shrug)." If being bored means being listless, then yes, I'm sometimes bored in the sense of lying back and letting the moments make themselves known. If being bored means being uninterested, then yes, I could say that I'm suitably bored at the age of 71, pleasantly bored, because I'm now entirely uninterested in being the most perfect or the best or the brightest. If that's being bored, then I am seriously bored, and pleased to be so.

⊫╪ ╪⊨

## COMING TO MYSELF

In the Bible story of the prodigal son, one translation says the wasteful son "came to himself", as though, in the midst of the confusion and dissipation of his life, he suddenly came face to face with his actual self, with who he truly was. The story often reminds me of a conversation I had years ago with a friend who was suffering a great sorrow. He said that, to his surprise, his sorrow had actually helped him understand who he was. He was a very successful teacher and devoted family man, and yet he said that only through this recent suffering had he gotten a glimpse of his true nature, and even a glimpse of the nature of reality itself. He said it seemed like he'd been blind all his life, and now, in the center of all this sorrow, he could suddenly see. I remember that something in his eyes seemed resplendent when he said that, and he smiled like a man re-made, which astonished me, because he was stretched in pain on a hospital bed as he spoke. Like the prodigal son, his anguish had somehow shown him the way to his true self. Strange, that, now in my 70s, I'm still searching for my true self. I'm sure it will be something surprising, and perhaps beautiful, when I finally find it. When I do, I'll think of the reborn Bible son, and my suffering but thankful friend.

⊫╪ ╪⊨

## DUST IN VAST WINDS

Somewhere in his book in the Bible, Job says that the words of his wise friends are no more significant than "proverbs of ashes", and it has me thinking, this morning, about the millions of words I spoke to my students, and how, years later, they're something like dust in the limitless universe of learning. I usually saw myself as a fairly sensible and shrewd instructor as I spoke to my students, but now, looking back, my words in the classroom seem like specks of small thoughts in a sky that goes on forever. The supposedly smart sentences I spoke in class and the lessons I set forth with self-assurance are now simply infinitesimal waves in the endless ocean of my students' education. Strangely, this is not a sad thought for me, but an inspiring one, for it reminds me of the immensity and majesty of the teaching-and-learning process that I was lucky to be part of for 45 years. I was just one of the countless teachers my students had, including their families and friends and the books they read and the people they spoke to in passing and the sights they saw and all the words they listened to in their young but limitless lives. Their teachers were as numerous as the stars in the sky, and my spoken words just happened to be among them, just happened to float through their rising lives for a few months and then drift off like dust in the vast winds of learning. I feel blessed to have been even a small part of such a grand and splendid process.

❧ ☙

### BEING LIKE THE WORLD

In a conversation with Jean Sibelius in 1907, the composer Gustav Mahler said that "a symphony must be like the world . . . it must embrace everything," and it occurs to me that the same could be said of one's life. Last summer, Delycia and I went up to Tanglewood to hear Mahler's 3rd Symphony, and the big-hearted music did, indeed, seem to hold in its arms both the loveliness and disarray of the world. It was as though Mahler wanted to welcome *every-thing* into his symphony – the pleasures and triumphs of the world, but also the disappointments and sorrows. There were stretches of pure majesty in the music, but there were also moments when the sounds seemed to collide and explode, as the parts of our lives sometimes do. I remember thinking, as I listened, that I could be as welcoming in making my life as Mahler was in making his music. Maybe I could think of my days as small, special symphonies, into which all the satisfactions and disasters, all the fun and failures of life, can be welcomed. I could, in a strange way, be another Mahler, making my own magnanimous music each day, greeting the good and the bad and bringing it all somehow into a song – not as majestic, certainly, as Mahler's symphony, but just one guy's song about the sheer outlandishness of his little but beautiful life.

# ALL SORTS OF ALLELUIAS
(written just before Christmas)

There will be alleluias sung in churches and homes these next few days, and I'm sure I'll be singing a special sort of alleluia now and then. I am not a regular church-goer, but I often choose to silently say praises to the "Lord" that I have come to believe in – not the distant and bewildering god I knew as a boy, but the infinite Spirit of goodness and concord that controls this universe I live in. I see reasons for alleluias all around me, every day, every moment. The stoplights that flashed this morning so the traffic flowed safely along, the checkout woman at Target who smiled at us so sincerely, the furnace in our cellar that's now singing and sending up heat for us – all of these are reasons for rejoicing. My "god" is simple goodness – the goodness I saw today in the girl who said "excuse me" as she passed us in a store aisle, and the goodness I felt when a clerk kindly smiled and showed us the way to the Christmas section. It wasn't a star-sprinkled or saintly or pious kind of goodness, just the simple and sincere goodness that's cared for the human race forever. I said several silent alleluias as we shopped today – quiet praises for the generosity of the healthy and bountiful forces that flow through all things at all times, not just at Christmas.

⇒+ +⇐

## COMPOSURE AND GRACE

For several years, a friend has been fighting a fearsome illness, and every time I've seen him I've marveled at the strength and grace with which he is waging his war. He's a warrior in the best sense, a fighter who's using both bravery and patience to beat back the despair that might beset others in such circumstances. He seems strong in a peaceful way -- brave, but calm and quiet in his bravery. I sense a kind of valiant mildness making its way across the room to me when I visit him, and it makes me thankful to be there. It's strange, how the courage of someone else can cause some heroism to start up in ourselves – perhaps more ability to stand up to the scary things in life and softly but strongly say what needs to be said and do what needs to be done. My friend speaks quietly but there's daring and steadfastness in his voice. I consider myself lucky to just sit and listen.

⇒+ +⇐

## SILENT UPON A PEAK

"Then felt I like some watcher of the skies
When a new planet swims into his ken;
or like stout Cortez, when with eagle eyes
He stared at the Pacific – and all his men
Look'd at each other with a wild surmise –
Silent upon a peak in Darien."

-- John Keats, "On First Looking into Chapman's Homer"

I'm always hoping to more often feel what "stout Cortez" and his men felt on that "peak in Darien". Keats pictures them standing on a hill above the Pacific Ocean, staggered by the scene, and I would like to foster more of that kind of bewilderment and wonder in my life. Cortez and his men saw a startling sight, and every day – every moment – I am witness to scenes which, in their own special ways, are just as amazing. Hard as it is to remember during the sometimes wearisome routines of the day, the various circumstances that arise around me are as unique and mystifying as the Pacific Ocean, and really, the only suitable response to them is honest amazement. The life I share with Delycia is my "Darien", and wherever I happen to be is the "peak" where I can look "with a wild surmise" at the inscrutable magnificence of life. A "surmise" is a guess, a supposition, a hunch, and that's honestly all I have when it comes to understanding the things I see and experience. In the end, they're all complete conundrums to me. If you ask me to make clear the mystery of even the simplest circumstance – the look of lamplight on a table, the sound of a car coming past the house, the whole sky shining at 7:00 a.m. -- all I could do is make a hit-or-miss guess, a "wild surmise". A better response might be to stay respectfully silent, like the astonished explorer and his men.

***

## MIRACLES

"Why! who makes much of a miracle?
As to me, I know nothing else but miracles . . .
To me, every hour of the light and dark is a miracle."

-- Walt Whitman, "Miracles"

There are thousands of things I've never seen –stars over Asia, rivers in a rain forest, the sun setting on icy cliffs. I could prepare a long list of the marvels I have missed, and spend several days just counting sounds I'll probably never hear, places of splendor I'll never see. Of course, I could instead spend those days listing the little and large spectacles I've been lucky enough to witness. In fact, it would take me dozens of days, months maybe, to review the astonishing events that have flowed through my life day after day. Have they all been grand and glorious, like mountain sunrises? No, but they've all been miracles, from the dust that just now sits beside me on my desk in appealing patterns, to the way wind whips tree branches around on a fall day, to the two leaves that just fluttered past the window where I'm typing these words with my elderly but still lively fingers.

⊶⊷

## FATHER-MOTHER SUN

It's easy to understand how "connected" I am when I see the sunshine spreading across my wife's gardens on spring mornings, for it's the same sunshine that warms the whole world. We live in a small town, but we share the sun with limitless numbers of living things, sharing as closely as brothers and sisters. The light that lands on her daffodils also fills valleys in France, and the same sunshine that sometimes brings out our sunscreen starts trees setting out new leaves in China. I try to think of this when the world seems like a disjointed, straggling place. When I feel like a puzzled sightseer on an utterly undisciplined planet, I try to see, in my mind, all the many millions of us living our lives lit up by the same sun. It's like we're all the offspring of sunlight. We all need the sunshine to restore us each morning, and all of us – all seven billion of us – say thanks, in our own ways, when it does. It's like we're living in an infinitely large family that finds comfort together under a light that never leaves us for long, and that illuminates all of our lives in similar ways. Even in our most troublesome times, the sun stays with us like a father for brothers and sisters, like a mother making sure her children are sharing, as one, her unfailing light.

═══╬ ╬═══

## MEASURING THE IMMEASURABLE

Unfortunately, I continue to make the mistake of measuring and limiting my life. We can only measure something that is made of matter, and the qualities of life that are truly special are made of something far different than matter. Could I think, for instance, of measuring my love? Or can I imagine putting a tape measure to my ability to be kind, or weighing my friendliness on a scale? And what about my inner energy, my desire to live life to the fullest? Is that something that can be delineated and computed and catalogued? Can I say, when I reach a certain age, that I have used up, say, 78% of my enthusiasm about life? The fact is that the extraordinary things in life – the forces like gentleness and peacefulness and patience and goodness – defy all measurement and limitation. The courage that is part of my inner life literally has no limit, and therefore cannot be measured and defined. It is as boundless as the heavens – more so, even. Today some people may consider me "old", but the truly crucial aspects of Hamilton Salsich are as unused and spirited as a spring day.

═══╬ ╬═══

## DAYS OF ROYALTY

On some autumn days, there's almost nothing in nature that doesn't carry itself royally. It's as if there are crowns of glory on every tree and bush and scurrying squirrel. That may sound strange, since autumn is the time of the year when nature appears to be fading and saying farewell until springtime, but I do see a peculiar kind of majesty when I stand outside in October. Even with just a few glittering leaves left, many trees glow like the crowns of queens and kings, and even old shrunken shrubs and flowers present themselves with elderly stateliness. At that time of year, the squirrels in our yard seem as self-important as small emperors as they survey the land they now essentially own, and the birds at the feeder are almost statuesque as they take their meals in small, stately groups. And the sky! Somehow there's always solemnity above us in the fall, particularly in the typically slim, resplendent clouds. It's as though the sky is being especially silent and magnificent to honor this august and solemn season.

⚜

## DANCING ON A RACQUETBALL COURT

Not long ago, after working out at the Y with Delycia, I was waiting for her near the indoor racquetball courts, when suddenly she swept around a corner with one of her irresistible smiles and said, "Let's practice our swing moves in here." "Here" was one of the racquetball courts, and before I could present a protest, her friendly persuasion had me on the court and we were swaying and swinging where racquetballs usually fly. The only music was in our heads, and it must have been good, because our moves, I thought, were among our best ever. We were very new to dancing, and there were stumbles among our swings, but on that small racquetball court at the YMCA, we grew a little as smooth senior-citizen dancers.

⚜

## NAMING BREEZES

This thought came to me during yesterday's breezy hours: *What if we decided to give names to separate summer breezes?* I imagined myself seeing breezes pass through trees and saying, "Let's see . . . I'll name the breeze in the upper part of the oak tree Jimmy, and I'll name the breeze in the lower part Joanne, and now the breeze in the lower part has changed, so I'll have to rename it and ...." It would have obviously been an impossible task. The breezes yesterday were not separate entities, but were part of something vast, part of the wide wind that was blowing through Mystic, which was part of the immeasurable flow of winds across the earth. No one would seriously think of isolating and naming single breezes. I began to wonder, then, whether our habit of isolating and naming *any* so-called separate, individual parts of our cohesive and harmonious universe isn't equally foolish. It's strange, for instance, that the name "Hamilton Salsich" is used to actually *identify* me, as though I am a distinct and separate "piece" of the universe. In a way, that's as silly as saying, "Oh, there goes Julia" as a breeze passes across my shirt. The truth is that the person referred to as "Hamilton Salsich" is *not* separate, *not* isolated, *not* solitary, but is always an inseparable part of the single, endless universe. I think and feel and do things because the universe thinks and feels and does things. The great system of winds blows across the earth, moving the breeze in the trees beside our house, and the vast assembly of miracles called the Universe (which is my name for "God") dances in its smooth and ceaseless way, moving the life called "Hamilton Salsich". Don't get me wrong -- I like my name. I use it to make life convenient for me, but I realize, all the while, that, like all names, it's just a handy but basically meaningless label for something that can never be separated from the endless dance of which it is a small but very vital part.

⇥ ⇤

## DANCING WITH QUEENS AND KINGS

When Delycia and I were dancing last night at the Knickerbocker Café in Westerly (RI), I think we felt, at least some of the time, like seasoned, free-and-easy dancers. We're senior citizens with our share of physical imperfections, and we're fairly new students of dancing, but last night we were a couple of young, footloose friends, twirling around like teens set free. The band was a breezy and buoyant group who were obviously out to make a merry evening for themselves as well as the patrons. They blew and strummed and sang like queens and kings of their instruments, like they were out to set a record for wholeheartedness. They seemed to play with pure pleasure, and that's how we danced. We tripped on each other and bumped other couples, but even those mistakes were made with fervor. We smiled when we stumbled, and laughed when we lost our balance. All evening long, the band broke free, again and again, with their strong-willed music, and we made our own kind of getaway – two silver retirees swaying and swinging like life had just started.

# TAKING LIFE EASY

The old saying "take it easy" sometimes starts me wondering whether life could be "taken" in such a way – taken the way I might take a drink of water or a loved one's hand. Life is, after all, a gift, and surely it's good to take a gift in a sweet-tempered, considerate manner. Whatever way the gift of life offers itself – as washing the dishes, as feeling the pain of loss, as driving to Boston on the interstate, as facing a fear of the unknown – I should take it with the same sense of spontaneity and effortlessness I would show in taking a taste of a delicious dessert, or in taking a tailor-made walk with my wife.

### THE CITY OF MY LIFE

Sometimes, sitting in an airplane window seat at night above a brightly lit city, I've thought of what almost seems like another shining city, the city of my own life. Now and then, when I'm able to see my life from a distance, it seems to be lit-up with lights of all kinds.

Close up, my life often seems under-lit and cluttered, but, when I stand way back, it looks like there's serenity and a sort of luster in my hours and days. All the people, for instance, who come and go through my life are shining with their own hopes and worries – the shimmering lights of optimism as well as the pale lights of unease and sorrow. From a distance, the events in my life also seem to be sparkling in countless hues as they pass through my days and disappear. Some good, some bad, some just tedious – all the large and small episodes in my days, when I observe them from far off, seem to shine in their various ways. Somehow they all seem more effulgent than harmful, full of more brightness than distress. I sometimes pretend I'm on a mountaintop looking down at the valleys and hills of my life, and I realize, again, that this life of mine, this grand gift I was given 73 years ago, is indeed, a shining city for me, a spectacle of lights like I might see from a night sky over New York.

—◄┼ ┼►—

## STAYING CALM

"She [stays] calm, whatsoever storms
May shake the world."

—Alfred, Lord Tennyson, "Idylls of the King"

Sailing with my dad years ago, I understood what Tennyson meant when he wrote these lines. Dad was as calm in stormy seas as he was when the winds were softly wafting us along. He seemed to understand that nature knows only calmness, even when storms are swirling. I think he saw serenity in every aspect of nature – in whirling waves as well as in smooth seas – and a similar serenity seemed to spread out from inside him when he was sailing. I recall seeing a strange poise, an almost blissful stillness, in his face as he steered his small sailboat in rough weather. Perhaps he smiled during storms because he sensed the gentleness inside the winds, the secret quietness and lightness in the lifting and falling of the waves. I saw it in him, too – the mildness with which he maneuvered the boat, the almost neighborly way he met the strong winds and waves. Dad's long gone, but I still feel his calmness, his ability to be quietly brave no matter what -- and I'm still trying to learn how to do it.

⊷⊶

## A DAY ABOUT CLOUDS

Early this morning, I decided to make this day a day about clouds. The sky was streaked with clouds as we drove to the gym, so I suppose that might have been why I chose to work hard today to see what's special about clouds. Mostly, I decided to simply see the clouds more clearly, to consider them carefully, to maybe sit outside and just stare at these surprising shapes in the sky. After all, they're always capricious, slowly shifting and adjusting as they pass across us, restyling their colors in subtle ways, so perhaps I should pause occasionally to make a serious study of them. Perhaps I should sometimes stop doing, doing, doing, and simply sit and let the stately loveliness of clouds impress me for a minute or two on this day that will, for me, be all about clouds.

⊷⊶

## DAYS OF REVERENCE

The word "reverence" has to do with treating someone or something with respect and honor, and it strikes me that any day deserves this kind of treatment. As I sit with Delycia during breakfast with morning light slowly spreading across the yard, I feel a sense of amazement at the appearance, once again, of so many marvels. The sunshine, for instance, brings its blessings to us from billions of miles away, and on most mornings it makes our grass shine and the side of the house next door stand out like a sheet of silver. When I see the trees swaying in passing breezes, I wonder how many little and large movements I will see during the day – the sway of Delyica's arms as she walks through the house, the easy passing of cars along our street, the sudden rising of birds from a bush. All days are surely days for reverence, days to welcome and bow to and give a greeting of esteem and praise.

---

## SEEING THE KINGDOM

When I recall hearing a boy many years ago say, as he stared at an ant colony museum display, "There's a whole kingdom here!", it reminds me that there are kingdoms everywhere. Truly, this universe is a place of kingdoms more fanciful than those in fairytales. Today I happen to be surrounded by the kingdom of snowflakes, and tonight, perhaps, it will be the kingdom of stars and a sliver of moon. There are even kingdoms inside the toast and coffee I had for breakfast this morning – intricate kingdoms ruled by tiny but mighty molecules. Today, when my wife and I talk together, we will enter the empire of ideas, perhaps the grandest of all kingdoms. We will travel from thought to thought like searchers among the stars and planets, scouts in the far-flung territories of the mind. We'll seem to be sitting on the couch having a simple conversation, but we'll actually be far off – and happily so – in the vast and sovereign state of ideas.

---

## DEATH AND THE BALLPARK

After attending a memorial service for a dear friend recently, it seemed fitting that Delycia and I attended a minor league baseball game the next day. My friend was a devoted baseball fan, and I felt his presence beside us as we braved the chilly weather to cheer for his favorite minor league team. The stands were full of families, full of moms and dads and daughters and sons and grandparents of all ages, all seeming to feel the youthful spirit of a Sunday afternoon ball game. There was newness and freshness all around us, from the healthful faces of toddlers to the sparkling eyes of grandparents glad to be with their families. There was an abundance of life at the game, a rising up of its brightness and sparkle, a spilling over of its spirit – and it made me think of my friend. His physical presence was now gone from us, but somehow that seemed to have allowed the spirit of his kindness and courage to be even bigger and braver. It's as if death had done us the favor of releasing more life than ever. I felt it at the baseball stadium that day, as if my friend's full life, along with the lives of the families finding joyfulness at a Sunday afternoon game, was overflowing around us.

⇒╪ ╪⇐

### LIKE FLOWERS

Delycia and I have been reading *The Education of Henry Adams* together, and I was thrilled today to read that Adams enjoyed working with his Harvard students because sometimes "their minds burst open like flowers at the sunlight of a suggestion." His metaphor made me see, for a moment, the millions of students whose minds, every so often, will be unfolding in fresh ways in their classrooms this year. There will be classrooms full of youthful, flourishing minds everywhere, minds made for the sole purpose of blossoming with bright new thoughts – and the slightest suggestion from a teacher can start the process. In these first weeks of my retirement from the middle school classroom, I will daydream, now and then, about these gardens of good young minds and their teachers. I will see students stretching and spreading out like the flowers in

Delycia's garden, and teachers trying their best to stay abreast of all this full-of-life sprouting and blooming. I won't miss it, because my wife and I will be doing our own special blossoming, but I'll see it in my daydreams sometimes.

⊷⊶

## LIVING A THOROUGH DAY

It would be a delight, now and then, to live a totally "thorough" day, one in which I do each activity as carefully and completely as possible. When I wash my face in the morning, I would do it in a soft but scrupulous way, being sure the soap does its work completely. Having breakfast with Delycia, I would savor the fragrance of my tea, and taste the toast in a meticulous manner, making each bite a sort of small ceremony. If I walked in the yard, I would walk with awareness -- with attention, perhaps, to the types of breezes passing by, or to the look of a cloud carrying itself lightly above the house. When reading, I would watch each word do its special work, each sentence spin its meaning. I would turn every page like it's precious, on this delightful day of thorough and devoted activity.

⊷⊶

## DEEP

When someone said to me, speaking about someone else, "He's really deep", I said to myself, "Yes, and aren't we all?" In 70+ years, I haven't met anyone who wasn't deep, in the sense of being a thoroughly impenetrable puzzle. Yes, I sometimes take satisfaction in saying I understand this or that person, but it's always a pretense, a charade that charms me into believing I am smarter than I actually am. In some places the ocean can be many miles deep, but not nearly as deep as every single person I pass on the street. There's eventually a bottom to the ocean, but where is the bottom

64

of someone's inner life – someone's sorrow, for instance? Where is the bottom of a broken heart, or of happiness? Is it ever possible to understand the scope of the most ordinary person's simple gladness? The Grand Canyon is deep, yes, but not nearly as deep as Corrine next door, or Chuck, the check-out guy at Stop-and-Shop. I stand in awe on the shore of any ocean, yes, but I should do the same in the presence of any person.

⇥ ⇤

# DOING A GREAT WORK

One day, as my grandson was working on a Lego project with single-minded passion, he paused and said to me, "I am doing a great work, Hammy", and I said to myself, *Yes you are, and so is everything.* The universe itself is an endless system of great works, from the falling of a single snowflake to the movements of the far-flung stars. These words I'm writing are doing the great work of wrapping thoughts like gifts to give away, and the cars I hear on a nearby highway are heading somewhere on great missions, from finding a good cafe to saving a loved one's life. We're all engaged in grand enterprises. Our smallest thought, if we only realized it, requires earnest labor, and being able to type a single word is a little miracle. It's a great work to give a greeting to someone, or to notice the sunshine on a sidewalk, or to set one foot in front of another, or to help hundreds of Lego pieces fit perfectly together.

## EARLY COLORS

Driving through coastal Connecticut on a day in May, Delycia and I were impressed by the colors in the early leaves and blossoms on the trees. We both said we had never noticed so clearly the soft pastel shades of trees in the first weeks of spring – the pale pinks and crimsons and light grays and even subdued shades of white. The trees looked like sprays of the softest crayon colors – tall bouquets of softness spread out along the roads. It was astonishing to me that never before in my 70-some springs had I noticed these understated nuances of color in the blossoming trees. I marveled at what I had missed, and I wondered, as I drove along, what other miracles had worked their wonders around me without my knowledge. What marvels had unfolded before me that I never noticed? And are they still happening constantly, like the sunlight that spreads around me in the morning, the air that effortlessly lifts my lungs, and the words that sometimes seem to write themselves on my computer screen?

━━╪╪━━

## EASY DOES IT

As my many years in the classroom passed, I gradually made increasing use of the long-standing slogan "Easy Does It". It was an advantageous change for me, because for the first half of my teaching career I could have honestly worn a button proclaiming "Hard Does It". In those early years, I approached teaching more like a warrior than an educator. Every aspect of teaching seemed to involve an obstacle to be overcome, a resistance to be neutralized, an enemy to be beaten. It was hard work – "hard" meaning tense, frenzied, and sometimes downright distressing. Thankfully, though, around my 15th year in the profession, I began to approach my work more like a sailor at sea than a soldier. When I was teaching, I often thought of my father, the finest sailor I knew and the man who taught me that "easy does it" on the high seas. Sailing was fairly easy, he said, if you simply let the wind do the work. He taught me not to fight the wind, not to try to control it or manipulate it or resist it, but simply to work with it. Fighting the wind was hard work; cooperating with it, combining forces with it, was, according to Dad, as easy as breathing. In the last decades of my 45-year teaching career, I often thought of him as I steered my lessons through 48-minute class periods. Like the whimsical winds of the ocean, problems and distractions arose and spun around me, but – remembering Captain Pete – I tried to relax and lighten up instead of stiffen and fight. As student questions were asked and comments were made, I turned the lesson a little this way or that to take advantage of the energies and interests in the classroom. This doesn't mean teaching became easy for me – just that I *took it easy* as I was teaching. There were times when I had to be firm with a student or a class, just as a sailor must pull hard on the sails or the tiller in a storm – but I tried to be firm in a gentle manner, strong in a considerate way. Dad always said a good sailor is both forceful and easy-going, both unyielding and laid-back – an approach that seemed to work as well in Room 2 as on Long Island Sound.

⊨⊨ ⊭⊨

## A TEACHING KIND OF LIFE

After my final graduation ceremony at the school where I taught for 35 years, a surprising thought came to me: *Now I can begin being a full-time teacher.* The sky was clearing after days of storms, and my mind seemed to be clearing also – seemed to be seeing previously unseen and somewhat startling possibilities. Teaching, it seemed for those few moments, doesn't have to happen only in a classroom with students, but can be a thread all throughout a "teaching kind of life". This kind of life involves teaching *all the time*, and with the same steadiness with which I breathe and think. This type of teaching is not just how to read and write, but how to live a loyal and lighthearted life. I realized, as I drove home from graduation with Delycia, that I was starting a new kind of teaching career -- as a street instructor, so to speak, a moment-by-moment mentor, a casual kind of coach, a tutor who takes on students anytime and anywhere. In the years to come, I knew I could teach in countless ways -- by talking courteously to a store clerk, by picking up something someone dropped, by listening with honest interest to anyone anywhere. Most importantly, I could teach *myself* by treating each moment as both a puzzle and a playful partner. I could prepare lesson plans on how I can praise each hour. I could lecture myself on letting go and lightening up. I could give myself quizzes on caring and sharing.

I knew on that final graduation day that my new classroom could be our couch or a street corner or the silent seashore at night. In this new career, I could live and teach like my lungs lift and fall, steadily and necessarily.

# ENJOYING THE GRAND CANYON

I t's so strange to me that still, in my 70's, I stress and fret over dozens of details each day, as though I'm the great master-creator, and the success of the day depends solely on me. That's about as silly as saying that I'm responsible for the sunshine I see outside today, or that sunset won't take place tonight unless I oversee the details. This universe is a spectacle of immeasurable proportions, and I am simply one of its numberless parts. It's not my duty to plan and present the spectacle, but simply to take pleasure in it and be blessed by it. Surely, if I were standing at the rim of the Grand Canyon, I wouldn't be fretting over some rocks that seem out of place, or stressing about shadows that don't appear as perfect as they should be. The Grand Canyon is glorious without any help from me, and so is all of life. Yes, I need to do my daily duties with care, but I also need to occasionally step back in astonishment and simply be grateful for the stunning spectacle called life. All of us are little Grand Canyons, suffused with mostly-undiscovered magnificence, and perhaps, every so often, we should set aside our fretfulness and unease and just sit and stare at our lives with fascination and thankfulness.

⇒+ +⇐

## WELCOMING THOUGHTS

Delycia and I welcome people into our home every so often for tea or dinner, and I am realizing that I should be more welcoming to the thoughts that move through the home of my mind. A steady line of thoughts constantly passes through my life, and I want to learn to welcome them all, even those filled with fear or dismay or discouragement. What I am slowly understanding is that my thoughts are not me, but fairly frail and short-lived whispers that will slip smoothly away *if* I just stand aside, observe them in a welcoming way, and then let them quietly leave. I could welcome thoughts of fear, for instance – politely listen to them, let them take their time passing through, and then see them to the door and down the road. I'm learning that thoughts are as harmless as I allow them to be – simply evanescent voices that will soon disappear if I stand by with something like a smile.

⇒+ +⇐

## A LUCKY HEIR

In terms of dollars, I don't have money to burn, but in terms of real riches, I am a wealthy man. I am actually an heir – a beneficiary of assets that can never be exhausted. I have access, 24/7, to funds that can keep my life continually healthy and happy. These funds are not dollars, not coins or cash or any kind of material currency. No, my wealth is the wealth that all of us share – the wealth of intangible (and therefore inexhaustible) qualities like caring and calmness and quietness and patience. Like all of us, I have a bottomless "bank account" of these qualities. I can withdraw them at any time, and amazingly, the account instantly refills with *more* than I withdrew. I get wealthier with kindness the more I spend it, and patience produces more patience the more I practice it!

———

## PASSION AND COMPOSURE

I am slowly becoming more skilled at working and resting at the same time, something I often see in nature. Trees, for instance, seem to be busily working when they sway in a strong wind, tossing their limbs in a spirited manner, but they also seem absolutely stress-free. Perhaps their secret is that they don't resist, but simply settle back and let the wind do the work, allowing them to sway tirelessly for hours. I see a similar situation in the autumn, when leaves offhandedly float to the ground in an effortless way and in a few days completely cover square miles of land with their colors. This is an astonishing achievement, one that would take we humans a supreme effort, and yet the loose and untroubled leaves do it in an almost leisurely way. And of course there are snowfalls, perhaps the most restful of nature's activities, with whole crews of snowflakes working in perfect peacefulness across the landscape. Within a few hours, a sovereign state of snow can set itself up across a landscape, and it does it in the quietest possible way. A snowstorm has a way of combining effort and restfulness, something I greatly admire. Perhaps my goal in life should be to live like snowflakes live, with both passion and composure.

———

## EPIPHANIES

One definition of an epiphany is "a moment of sudden revelation or insight", something that I'm sure happens to all of us more times than we realize. I've had thousands of epiphanies over the last 70+ years, everything from suddenly realizing, one April day back in 7th grade, that I was in deep trouble with Sister Virginia Marie, to unexpectedly understanding, one morning, how to securely install a bracket for a flag to an outside wall. I suppose we have these epiphanies almost constantly – these sudden understandings, unforeseen eye-openers, "aha!" moments that make some part of life instantly comprehensible. Strangely, one of my most common epiphanies is the out-of-the-blue understanding that I don't really understand much of anything – that this life is ultimately a beautiful but unsolvable mystery, of which I am a small but essential part. These are instructional epiphanies that, in a flash, make clear to me my safe and lucky place in this hugely puzzling but relentlessly perfect universe. I'm always grateful when they make what have become their regular daily visits.

━╬ ╬━

### EVERYDAY CHANTS

When Delycia and I were visiting a retreat center, we listened to some chants one morning – not call-and-response chants like the "kirtan" we participated in the previous night, but just the usual chants of day-to-day life. A chant is essentially a repetitive rhythmic phrase, and they were everywhere that morning. As Delycia and I walked up and down the grassy lawns for exercise before breakfast, every bird's song was a chant, the same smooth phrases sung over and over. Then, at the customary silent breakfast, there was a soothing kind of chant-like rhythm in the sounds in the otherwise silent dining room – shoes shuffling, silverware clicking, glasses clinking. It seemed, as I listened, more and more like a chant chosen just for all of us who came to the retreat center for comfort and understanding. And even later, as I was writing in the downstairs reception area, I heard chants of laughter around me, small volleys of gladness in seemingly rhythmical patterns. There was an almost lyrical quality to the laughter – first some quiet conversation, then soft explosions of laughter, then more conversation, then laughter briefly bursting out again. It was like a chant of good cheer, this graceful flow of laughs, the kind of chant a writer like me can love as he's letting words loose in sentences.

⊨⊣ ⊢⊨

## AN EVERLASTING LIGHT

Whenever I hear the Christmas song about the little town of Bethlehem, I especially notice the phrase "the everlasting light", and it sometimes starts me thinking about the everlasting lights in my own life. One of these lights would be simple gentleness. What darkness can put out the light of gentleness? What sorrow can kill a person's gentleness, a person's ability to be tender toward others? True, in a tragedy it may appear that gentleness has disappeared in the smoke of misfortune, but shortly it always reappears, even more durable and undying than before. Gentleness can never be vanquished, because it's not made of bricks and mortar or bones and muscle or dollars and cents. Gentleness is like light: it looks soft, but it can shine through or around or over any problem. Gentleness is unobtrusive and sometimes unnoticeable, but, like light, it can instantly destroy the deepest darkness. Perhaps what was born in the dark manger many years ago was the inextinguishable light of gentleness. Perhaps that is what I, a non-churchgoer, worship at that special time of year.

⊨⊣ ⊢⊨

## SIGNALS?

I sometimes wonder if I'm missing certain special signals sent to me occasionally from here and there. Yesterday I was watching a tree as it turned and bent and bowed in the wind, its limbs and leaves lifting and falling, and, as silly as it might sound, it seemed like the tree was sending me signals. It was like small messages made just for me: "Are you there, Hamilton? Are you truly alert and listening to the sounds I'm making with this wind?" Then I saw a seagull sailing in circles above the tree, and I wondered if there were signals there also. Perhaps the bird was sending from the sky the news that nothing is better than right now: "Hammy, happiness is inside you, right there where you're sitting in the shade with a glass of ice water at 3:37 on a sweltering afternoon." Then, in the next instant, I found myself listening to the sounds of cars on the distant interstate, and they sent – in soft, almost whispery sounds – the message that I'm an amazing mystery. "You're astounding," they said, "and so is this afternoon and everyone and everything." It seems strange, I know, but I'll be searching for signals tomorrow, as well.

⊨╬ ╬⊨

## EVERYDAY BALLET

After Delycia and I saw a stunning performance by the Boston Ballet, I got to thinking, as we rode home on the train, that beautiful ballets are continuously being danced all around us. It's strange that I so often miss this marvelous fact – that dance-like harmonies of the highest order are everywhere, *always*. Closest to home, there's the graceful symmetry of our bodies – our balanced limbs and organs, as well as the flawless steadiness of the passing of blood through our veins and arteries. There's the graceful twirl of tree limbs in winds, the spins that sparrows show off as they search for food, and the stylish skips and leaps of squirrels. Even the slow fall of old blossoms to the grass seems to be done with poise and precision, as we saw on that day in Boston, where floating white dogwood petals pirouetted in the air around us as we walked through a park after the performance. Ballet at the theater is a blessing, but no more so than the skillful dancing of the every-day world.

# EVERYDAY MAGIC

I sometimes enjoy practicing magic tracks, but there's another kind of magic, more concealed and commonplace, a magic I can be grateful for every second of my life. The cells in my body, for instance, are constantly making magic in countless ways. Like tiny, multifaceted factories, they are continuously engaged in manufacturing complex molecules called proteins, and are steadily waging intricate battles against any "invaders" that might upset my body's mechanisms. Not only that, my cells are replacing and renewing themselves so fast and efficiently that I become almost a new person roughly every 7-10 years! That's a personalized, custom-made kind of magic that happens always and endlessly, and is far more fascinating than making a coin disappear in a tissue.

⇒‖⇐

## SIXTY DAWNS IN EVERY MINUTE
It's wonderful to awaken in the morning to a world that seems totally new -- completely full of freshness, loaded with bloom and

novelty, big with brand new blessings – but what's even more wonderful is to realize that this new, unblemished world is, in fact, with me every moment. *I actually cannot escape newness.* Strange as it sounds, oldness is really nowhere because newness is always everywhere. All I'm ever presented with is the pristine present moment, a moment never before known by me or by anyone. It may sometimes *seem* similar to my past moments – and this is what can make oldness seem so real – but actually, each moment is a groundbreaking, cutting edge creation, coming to me the way dawn does each morning. In each minute I have sixty seconds, sixty dawns, sixty new sensations, sixty chances to celebrate something novel and new-fangled. This, it seems to me, is cause for some smiles during the day, and occasionally even a spirited shout.

⊶ ⊷

## EVERYTHING WORKS

Sometimes small things don't seem to work in our house, so it's good to occasionally stand back and see, again, that the whole world actually *always* works flawlessly, in one way or another. If a window won't close easily, I could say it's working very well *as one of my teachers,* telling me to take my time and stay patient when problems arise. If the flow of water from our well slows somewhat while I'm showering, the good news is that it slows simply because it's working in perfect rhythm with the condition of the water table beneath us. If a light switch won't switch on, it's working quite nicely as a reminder to stay serene and let small problems pass by like the breezes sometimes blowing outside our house, making trees sway in the most perfect ways.

⊶ ⊷

## A SINGLE ROUSING THOUGHT

It may seem strange to think of positive ideas as forces that can "fall" upon a person, but sometimes it does seem to happen, a thought

suddenly swooping down on me like sunshine that sweeps everything else away. It can create a newness and impressiveness in my
life, like a letting go of all that's old while something fresh flows in.
I'm one person one second, and then a thoroughly surprising idea
sweeps into my life, and suddenly I'm someone new, someone I've
never met. It feels like a mental flood has flowed through me, leaving something lighthearted and bright when it's gone. For instance,
occasionally this cheering idea drops down on me: *thoughts are more*
*powerful than things.* It's a simple concept, one that has occasionally restarted my life, this idea that a strongly held hopeful thought
can control and conquer any situation, no matter how menacing it
might seem. Each time I understand, once again, that the positive
thoughts inside me can speak with infinitely more force than any
troublesome circumstance outside me, I feel startlingly free, totally
fresh and remade. I feel reborn as a force, not of blood and bones,
but of soul and spirit, all because of a single rousing thought from
somewhere above and beyond.

⊷╌ ╌⊶

## IRREPRESSIBLE FLAMES

When I watch the fire in our fireplace on winter days, flowing
and flaring and sending up sparks, I often think it looks a lot like
my life. There's a sort of waywardness in the flames, a beautiful
disorderliness that seems similar to what I sometimes see in my
days. There's no pattern in the way the flames move, just as there
is often no noticeable pattern in the comings and goings of my
life. Flames flare and fizzle down again in random ways, just as
good and not-so-good things in my life flow in and flicker out with
perfect casualness. Occasionally, some glowing logs collapse with a
soft explosion, just as carefully proposed plans of mine sometimes
quietly crumble. But not to worry – when I put some new logs on,
the flames quickly curl up around them, just as, in my life, the
fires of new plans are always ready to flare up. It's interesting that

the flames in the fireplace seem almost irrepressible, as if they're managing themselves and making their own rules, springing up and spreading just as they wish. My life often looks like that, like a strange and astonishing assembly of flaring and flashing happenings. It occurs to me that I should perhaps watch my life with as much fascination as I watch the fire in our fireplace on frosty afternoons.

⇒═╪ ╪═⇐

## IN THE MIDDLE OF NOWHERE

Yesterday, a friend told me he was recently hiking in a forest and soon found himself, as he said, "in the middle of nowhere", and it reminded me of a somewhat strange hope I always have when I start reading a work of fiction. As surprising as it may sound, I hope I will feel sort of startled and dumbfounded by what I am reading, even somewhat lost inside the pages. If, when I'm reading a short story, I feel, for awhile, like I'm "in the middle of nowhere", I say good for me, for then I might have the stirring experience of finding my way to somewhere. We often forget that in order to experience illumination we have to first experience darkness, and that the contentment of new knowledge can only come after the discontent of confusion. If I'm never "in the middle of nowhere" when I'm reading a story, how can I ever feel the thrill of finding the somewhere of the story's heart? In a sense, reading fiction, for me, is about walking into darkness so I can better appreciate the light when it comes. For that reason, I guess I didn't especially enjoy the "easy" novels I have read – novels that were filled, you might say, with easily noticeable light – because in those books very little finding, uncovering, or stumbling upon was possible. I take the most pleasure in novels that puzzle me with their shadows and obscurity, in stories that sometimes conceal their meanings in an exciting kind of darkness, because then, there's always the possibility of some sudden and even spectacular light ahead.

⊨⊹⊨

## INFINITE ABILITIES

I recall a friend once telling me that the weather has what he called "infinite abilities" to surprise us. He said there's no limit to what the weather can do, because it doesn't grow weak and weary like we do. This morning I was thinking about what he said, and it started me wondering if we, too, might actually have some infinite abilities – the ability, for instance, to bring some brightness to others, or the ability to be brave when life breaks down, or the ability to believe in kindness when cruelty seems in control the world over. I, for one, am weary of the limiting outlook on life – the view that we can have only so much satisfaction or whole-heartedness or amazement, that these qualities come only in small quantities and will sooner or later shrink away. I've known people who paid tribute to the good gift of life even when suffering severely, even when hope seemed to hold out no hand. Was their cheerfulness and inner liveliness limited? Did they see their supply of benevolence as being insufficient, restricted, scanty? To them – and to me – a quality like the ability to be amazed by the beauties of this universe is without limits. When the door of death swings open for me, I hope I'm able, even then, to be astonished by the mysteries of all things. I hope I can still shout, at least in spirit, some words of praise for the gifts I'm given each moment.

⊨⊹⊨

## FLIPS, SNAPS, FLICKS, AND WHISKS

Each winter morning, just a quick tap on the thermostat sets the flow of warm air from the furnace flowing. Then a flick of a switch sends light into the bathroom, and a twist of a faucet starts water shooting into the sink. Later, a quick click opens the teapot, and a push on a button soon brings the water to a boil. Soon I quickly flip my eggs, the toast pops up, and breakfast is whisked off to the sunroom, where two friends click with each other while birds swish and shake around the feeder.

# FREELY RECEIVED,
# FREELY GIVEN

I don't do much community service work, but I do often have a feeling of "giving back". I'm not sure where it comes from or why it keeps flowing into me, but I have been on the receiving end, over 74+ years, of a river of ever-new thoughts. It seems to me that I don't actually make these thoughts, but that some other power helps them unfurl and continuously cascade through me. Just sitting here now, holding my hands to the keyboard, countless thoughts from somewhere are showing me what words to type. Since all these mental gifts have been so freely given to me, I take pleasure, day by day, in freely re-giving them to my friends and acquaintances. Because they belong to the limitless universe of thoughts, they're not mine to keep, and so sending them straight on to others seems like the suitable next step. I sometimes see myself as a kind of strange Santa Claus carrying a big bag of thoughts which came my way by some incomprehensible good luck, and which I distribute to others with the cheerfulness of an old and lucky guy.

◄┼ ┼►

## GAPS

It often occurs to me that I need more "gaps" in my life. According to one dictionary, a gap is simply "an unfilled space or interval", and I am certain I would appreciate more of those during my sometimes headlong hours and days. Surely I would be grateful for an occasional chance to choose "nothing" as an activity – to neither listen nor speak nor think, but just sit in ease and stillness. In the midst of the steady streams of thoughts and words that swirl through my life, I would welcome the possibility of easing up, slowing down, and sometimes just simply stopping. It's strange that I don't realize this more thoroughly, and put it into practice. How hard is it to understand that gaps – interludes when nothing happens – are an essential aspect of all lives? Don't we take pleasure in the long gaps every night in which we settle and refresh our lives through sleep? And aren't there ever-so-brief gaps between the words we speak, between the breaths we take, between the beats of our hearts? Why, then, do I so often insist on living a gapless life, shoving myself ahead in a nonstop manner, breathlessly pushing myself toward endless finish lines? What about an occasional pause to seriously consider what's been said? What about stopping to actually *think* about my thoughts? What about a deep breath now and then?

◄┼ ┼►

## GETTING OUT OF PRISON

I got to thinking today about how refreshing it is to free oneself from the prison of resentment. I'm not sure why, but I was remembering an incident from many years ago when, having felt injured by someone's remarks and having enclosed myself in bitter resentment for awhile, I was suddenly able to free myself from it. I'm not sure why or how, but I surprisingly broke down the walls of my own anger and, in my heart, completely forgave the person. I remember it so well, the feeling of unqualified freedom that came over me. I was released from the prison of my own resentment. I was free to accept and even be at ease with the remarks that had so hurt me. I saw the remarks as if from a great distance, and they seemed as harmless as birds flying far away. And now it has me wondering: Could I perhaps forgive other so-called harmful things, even things like serious illness, or tragedy? If these happen, could I forgive them, and thus rise up out of the prison of fear and anger and bitterness? Would this help me to see illness and tragedy as simply events in my life, events with which I can be comfortable instead of angry, events that could release me into the freedom of acceptance instead of confining me in the prison of hostility?

---

## SPECIAL CRAYONS

Some days, I feel like my pockets are full of enchanted crayons that can color the world in beautiful ways. Of course, it doesn't really need coloring, since all things, even the smallest stick in the grass or the faintest shred of a cloud in the sky, shine with assorted hues of color, but sometimes it's fun to feel like a kid again and pretend to color my days like they're pages in a coloring book. Most days can be made to seem vivid and vibrant, and I take pleasure in pretending that I'm the artist. I swish my crayons across hours of gray rain, and what I see then is hours of softness and freedom for me. I color a tedious meeting with various shades, and suddenly there's something stirring in the words we participants speak. I use "sky blue" and "melon" on some strenuous duties, and step back and see the secret rewards in them. It sometimes takes just a second to swipe some colors across a person or a situation, and notice, however faint, something beautiful. It doesn't always work, but in a world that often seems stained with confusion and sorrow, it's worth a try.

⊷ ⊶

## DEATH AND BIRTH IN THE GARDEN

I guess I must have known this, but for some reason I found it somewhat astonishing when Delycia told me yesterday that daylilies actually bloom for only a single day. All that work, I thought -- all those frozen February weeks, then all those spring and summer days of patiently pushing up through soil and air – all that for just a few short hours of splendor! As she was speaking, I was looking at a particularly remarkable yellow lily near us, and found it startling to realize it would be colorless and shriveled tomorrow. For a few minutes, as we often do, we strolled among her good-looking lilies, admiring the intense and almost furious colors of some, as if they were softly shouting at us about how handsome they were on this single day of their lives. It seemed strange, as we walked, that these beautiful blossoms would wither and waste away by the morning, but I couldn't help thinking, too, that that's also sort of the glory of life – that things are continually leaving us so that others can come and take their places. New lily blossoms are born each day, but only because yesterday's blossoms bowed down and departed, and new lives of all kinds arrive among us because old lives give up the gift of living. We see death each day in Delycia's garden – the death of dozens of beautiful blossoms – but precisely because of the deaths, we also see, each morning, the delivery of dozens of new blossoms, fresh and mint-condition miracles of color. I guess it's part of the strange magnificence of our lives on this planet, that death, the most feared of all our foes, is what opens the door to life.

⊷⊶

## GLAD ALL MY DAYS

Riding home from New York City on the train one Saturday with Delycia, returning from seeing an opera at Lincoln Center, I found myself thinking I should be glad all my days – not glad because great things are always happening (because they're not), but glad for the gifts found, somehow and some way, in each moment. When I feel my life leading me from one problem to another, I can actually, strange as it may sound, be glad for the gift of the problems, since problems can shine like useful lights. In the midst of sorrow, I can be glad that a good breath of air is brought to my lungs each moment, and that a new morning always follows night. When a day seems more dark than light, I can at least be glad that I have eyes that can see both the darkness and the little but beautiful light.

⊷⊶

## GLORY

"Glory be to God" is a phrase I often heard growing up, but some mornings I think about glory be to overflowing flower gardens, and glory be to blue skies, and glory be to a good cup of tea. I don't regularly attend church, but I do worship the wonders of this world. I praise the power of a few flowers to stay strong on frosty mornings, and I praise the power of my hands that help me write these words. I give homage to the holy eggs which sizzle on our stove each morning, and I give kudos to cranberry jam and the juice of green grapes. I say glory be to the greatness of this moment, and to the majesty of our small house in Mystic, and to the magnificence of the birds on our feeder day after glorious day.

# NEWS TO TELL ON A
# MOUNTAIN

During a holiday concert several years ago by the Coast Guard Academy Band, the soloist sang "Go Tell It on the Mountain", and it made me also want to tell a few things on some mountain. From her mountain, the soloist wanted to say the good news that Jesus was born, but I want to say some other, less celebrated good news. I want to say, for instance, that there's far more love in the world than malice; that the sturdy, stretched-out arm of sincerity is stronger than deceitfulness; that the greatness and power and glory of life is in kindheartedness, not in acrimony; that the some-times destructive "wisdom" of the adult world is, thankfully, utter foolishness to children; that the invisible things of life (like love) are more wonderful than the visible; that the spirit of apprecia-tion is more uplifting than the spirit of gossip; that, if we open our eyes and hearts, we can know the things that are freely given to us by love; that goodness, not money, makes a person mighty; that the power of kindness can shatter fears; that compassion always conquers cruelty; that cheerfulness always defeats defeatism; and that gentleness was and is and will be, forever. Maybe I should find a mountain somewhere and start climbing.

⊷ ⊶

## GOLD FREELY GIVEN

Mowing the lawn one morning in October, I came upon some golden leaves spread beneath one of our birch trees, and when I was finished mowing, it started me searching for other unnoticed golden surprises. I sat in a lawn chair in the backyard and simply started looking around for gold and its likenesses. Within seconds, I saw the golden stripes on the peace flag that was flying from the trellis over one of our gardens, and then the golden zinnias beneath it, and then the clouds of golden daisies beside the house. Soon I seemed encircled by gold -- by lilies and sunflowers and speckled sunlight on grass and even the pale golden sides of our neighbor's house. And finally, as I was finishing my search, I saw the flash of the wings of four goldfinches fluttering around one of our feeders. It was a golden few minutes for me, a gift freely given to an old guy who gives thanks for a golden life.

⊷ ⊶

## GOOD CONFUSION

I've come to see, as my 70-some years have passed, that confusion can be good for me – that it gives me more gifts than problems. Perhaps that shouldn't be surprising, since the word "confuse" derives from the Latin word for "mingle together", and aren't all things in this world mingled together, in some way or other, and isn't mingling usually a constructive activity? Grass blades make fine-looking lawns by growing in a confused way, all mingled to-gether, and the stars above us show the beautiful confusion of togetherness and endlessness. Cars on roads mingle in a seemingly confused manner, and yet the chaos of the traffic – what we might call the resourceful confusion of it – usually produces a steady and smooth movement of vehicles. My days, too, so often seem composed of haphazard things and thoughts, and yet from that confusion has come, and still comes, the blessings given by this good life. It's a similar confusion, I guess, to that of oceans that bring beauty out of swirling waves and organisms, or of fields of wildflowers that show splendor in the midst of seeming disarray. It's a lucky kind of confusion, and I'm lucky to usually be feeling it.

⇥ ⇤

## A SHOWER EVERY SECOND

Sometimes I start the day with a shower, but actually, every single moment starts with a cleansing shower of sorts. After all, each moment is made right here, right now, absolutely new, and therefore fresh and spotless. No matter how tired and tedious life can sometimes seem, each second actually spreads out in an upsurge of unreserved newness. Oldness is only in my mind, not in what's made moment by moment. I sometimes think thoughts of oldness, but even those thoughts are as unblemished as a sunrise. No moment in the past was exactly like this one, and therefore this one rises as a new-made miracle, just out of the freshening shower of the universe.

⇥ ⇤

## GOOD GROUND

When April is set to show us some sunshine and warm weather (we hope), I think of seeds and the sort of ground they need in order to sprout up and succeed – not just the seeds of plants, but the seeds of a good life as well. Just as the seeds of flowers will prosper if the soil is in good shape, so will the seeds of a promising life unfold and thrive when planted in a generous and nourishing heart. Rock-strewn soil won't promote the growth of new grass, and neither will a closed and complaining mind make it easy for happiness to take root. Each spring in Mystic, flowers will flourish only in good ground, and inspiring feelings will unfold only in bright and spacious hearts.

—━┥ ┝━

## DANCING ONE STEP AT A TIME

"Honesty, truth-telling fairness, was Mary's reigning virtue: she neither tried to create illusions, nor indulged in them for her own behalf, and when she was in a good mood she had humor enough in her to laugh at herself."

-- George Eliot, *Middlemarch*

If people could see me when I'm alone, they might be surprised by the fact that I often seem to be laughing. It's not an uncommon occurrence for me. I regularly find myself almost folded over in laughter when I'm alone, and it's usually directed at myself. I often cannot believe some of the silly, self-promoting, and completely incomprehensible things I say and do in a day's time, and it doesn't deserve anything but a good laugh. Looking back on a day, it's as if I'm sitting in the audience at a comedy show, and my strange shenanigans that day make up the show. I don't mean to suggest that I'm a complete catastrophe as a human being, but I do seem silly to myself when I'm pridefully prancing around like some shrewd mastermind. I know a little about the laws of good writing and how to choose deli items for dinner and when to write a note in the margins of novels, but there are thousands of things I know nothing about. No one is less of an "authority" than I am. I suppose I'm sort of an expert at using commas correctly, but I'm a downright dimwit when it comes to correctly carving a turkey or turning a lawn into a lavish garden or giving the right gifts to my grandchildren. This is the reason for my occasional amusement at myself when I'm alone. I just have to laugh at this well-creased senior citizen who gives off such a sense of self-assurance and as-tuteness, but who is actually dancing one clumsy (albeit spirited) step at a time.

⇥ ⇤

## SETTING HAPPINESS FREE

Strange as it may sound, I want to do more releasing than grasping, and it will be a satisfying shift for me. I've spent far too much time trying to grasp and hold onto happiness, and it's been a wearying kind of work. I'm tired of struggling to seize peace and well-being, to grab this bit of gladness or that bit of pleasure, as if happiness is something tangible that can be caught and kept. I want to live in a different way. I want to set my good fortune free instead of grasp-ing and clutching it. I've had sadness in my life, for sure, but I've also been blessed with a bounteous supply of happiness, and in-stead of trying to hold onto it, I want to give it its natural freedom. I want to release my cheerfulness so it can cheer up other lives. I want to liberate the delight I've been lucky enough to receive so it can loosen and free up others. I'm tired of clutching and clinging to happiness. I want to allow it to leave so it can spread its gifts around. (Surprisingly, that's the only way I can be sure it will stay with me.)

⇥ ⇤

## GREAT LIGHTS

I was struggling recently with some puzzling passages in a book, when suddenly it was as if something illuminated the sentences and I was able to quickly and clearly see their meanings. To me, it was a startling illumination after many minutes of confused reading and re-reading. It seemed like a light had been given to me from somewhere. It started me wondering: How does it happen that all of a sudden some mystifying words on a page can shine with significance? Why does the light of understanding sometimes suddenly switch on where there was, moments ago, only obscurity and confusion? I guess I shouldn't be surprised, because this kind of sudden shining occurs in my life fairly often. As I was writing this, I could see the old quilt of snow across our yard, and even after many weeks and under gray skies, it still glowed with surprising brightness. It was as if long, glowing light bulbs were laid out beneath the snow, bringing a luminous brilliance up to the surface. What's interesting is that I almost never notice this brightness in old snow cover, just as I often don't see the meanings in sentences set down in a book. I guess it takes some stroke of magic to make both month-old snow and perplexing sentences abruptly light up for this old but still wholehearted fellow.

# HAM'S CASTLE

I think I need to get a larger outlook on life, since I sometimes don't seem to have room enough to receive all the gifts I get each day. Perhaps I need to see my life as a vast castle that can easily hold the endless gifts I'm given, gifts like the sunlight that's almost always with me, and the eyesight that allows me to look at the light shining on slowly vanishing snow, and the wind that whips up fresh weather second by second, and the full-of-life thoughts that arise inside me by the thousands each day. Perhaps my life should be called "Ham's Castle", a palace with no walls and no doors, a mansion that widens whenever necessary to welcome the crowds of gifts that constantly surround it, asking for entrance.

⚊⚊

### HIDDEN WORDS AND WONDERS
Not long ago, as the dentist was working on my teeth, I studied some hidden-word puzzles on the ceiling, and soon, as the drill droned on, I was thinking of other hidden surprises in my life, the

little wonders that wait by the thousands for me to find them. As I thought about it, it seemed possible that all the moments in a day are made of useful surprises, small shocks that have the power to uplift a life. A day could be compared to a puzzle in which wonders wait beneath the seemingly humdrum happenings. I thought perhaps I could be like a scout searching a wilderness of secret treasures. As the dentist did his work, my day-to-day life started to seem like a stirring escapade, a journey among unseen jewels and gems. They were just words hidden among letters on the dentist's ceiling, but they helped me have a look into the fortune-filled life I'm lucky to be living, even when I'm lying back in a dentist's chair.

⊷ ⊶

## A NEW REALIZATION

This morning, as I was reading in the New Testament about Paul's "conversion" – how, as I understand it, he suddenly came to a completely new way of thinking about love – I realized that I need to think, again, about what love actually is. First of all, perhaps I should capitalize the word, to show that it stands for a force that is totally non-material, and that therefore has no limits and can never be destroyed or even slightly diminished. This is perhaps what Paul saw on the road to Damascus – that this power called love, or Love, is not confined to any particular place or object, but is worldwide, widespread, and invincible. Having no material boundary lines, there's no place where Love isn't present, and there's no power that can oppose its preeminence. What's extraordinary about this is that the same is true for other non-material qualities. Kindness, for instance, has no boundaries and can never be even slightly restricted by any material force. Enthusiasm, too, cannot be confined or constrained, for it is made of nothing but its own wholehearted spirit. Gentleness, confidence, generosity, peacefulness – all of these are intangible, elusive forces that sweep through the universe without hindrance. I suppose what really astonished Paul about his new realization is that it thoroughly transformed his notions about God. He had probably been trapped for years by the belief that the supreme being was some type of superhuman ruler who controlled the universe the way a human monarch would. What he suddenly saw on the road to Damascus was that this force called "God" was actually far, far greater than he had imagined. He now saw that it is a non-material and therefore boundless power that is utterly unassailable and indefatigable. It's the power of Love, the power that knocked this hostile persecutor of Christians right off his horse.

⇒╬⇐

## HOME

My wife and I have a small home beside a river in a small town, but I wish I could more often feel like I'm home no matter where I happen to be. Home is our white stone house in Mystic, but home should also be the sidewalk I'm walking on, or the store where I'm browsing among beets and cabbages, or the forest in which I'm walking on an April day. Home, as we say, is where the heart is, and shouldn't my heart be wherever I happen to be, whether at the beach beneath a few first stars or at a meeting that seems boring but that brings brightly-shining thoughts out from each of the participants, if only I could see and appreciate them? Shouldn't I feel just as "at home" holding the door for a friend miles from our house as doing the dishes in our kitchen, and shouldn't speaking to the clerk at a store be, in a way, as pleasant as passing thoughts back and forth at home? I live in little Mystic, but I also live in the limitless universe, so perhaps my real home is as vast as galaxies. It could be there are countless doors in my real home, all leading to moments that could be called miracles, all opening to places as comfortable and kindly as our living room on Riverbend Drive.

⊷⊶

## A PLACE OF HOLY MYSTERY

"They all realized they were in a place of holy mystery..."

--Luke 7: 16-17

When I read this sentence in the gospel of Luke this morning, I immediately thought of my classroom in the many years when I was teaching. It might seem odd to think of a small classroom in a quiet, unassuming school in southeastern Connecticut as being "a place of holy mystery". After all, it was a rather commonplace classroom, no different, really, than the thousands of other class-rooms in the country. Kids came and went, talking and yawning and trying their best to stay focused, not thinking much, I'm sure, about miracles and holy mysteries. For me, though, my little room at 89 Barnes Road was truly a sacred place, for I knew that miracu-lous things happened there. In this room, forty-two students and one teacher had their lives transformed each and every day, not because of especially good teaching, but just because that's the na-ture of this amazing process called "learning". When people come together to share ideas, lives are changed. It's the law. It always happens. I once calculated that approximately 500,000 thoughts occurred to my students and me in my classroom on a typical school day. Think of it – all those thoughts swirling together in my room, mingling and sharing and transforming! It's like a magic potion of ideas, and not one of us could avoid being changed by it.

Even if we were not especially tuned into what was happening on a given day, we couldn't help being transformed, at least somewhat, by the blending and stirring of ideas in my classroom. How did it happen? Why did it happen? I really have no idea. I planned my lessons and worked as hard as I could to be a good teacher, but I must honestly say I have no clue as to how this miracle called learning happens. I guess that's what made my classroom – and *any* classroom – "a place of holy mystery".

━━╬ ╬━━

## LUCKY TO BE OLD

I am old, and feeling lucky to be so, and liking it a lot. The word "old" is related to the Greek word "αλδαίνω", meaning "to strengthen", and I think old folks like me are sometimes stronger than in our younger days – not physically stronger, but stronger in our hearts and minds, better able to be brave in a sometimes ominous world. My biceps have broken down considerably, but my sense of dignity and self-respect is stronger than ever. My lungs don't lift and fall as smoothly as they used to, but my ability to be both audacious and serene has improved each year. The word "old" is related to the Latin word "altus", meaning "high", and I guess I'm proud to have reached the heights of old age, the peaks of seniorhood, the summits of advanced years, from where I can look out and see how lucky I am to be standing strong, high up and happy, old and getting older - and more grateful - each day.

━━╬ ╬━━

## PROUD TO BE IGNORANT

I have slowly come to see that ignorance is as necessary to learning as good soil is to a garden. Ignorance, you might say, is the fertile soil of first-rate education, for without it no learning would take place. I can't learn something unless I'm first ignorant of it – unless there is first an empty space in my understanding that can be filled by awareness and appreciation. It's surprising to me that so many people seem to want to hide their ignorance – to pretend that it doesn't exist. That's as foolish as hiding the soil of your flourishing flower garden because you're ashamed of it, or pretending the slimy mire of pond bottoms isn't actually the source of every handsome water lily blossom. Out of the darkness of night comes the light of morning, and out of the perplexity of ignorance comes the longed-for shimmer of insight. I'm proud to be, relatively speaking, overwhelmingly ignorant, because it means I have a universe of learning ahead of me.

⊰⊱

## HUNTING GOODNESS

Some friends of mine are serious hunters, and I guess I'm a sort of hunter, too. My friends hunt mostly deer, whereas I hunt mostly goodness. My friends probably stalk their prey in a silent and serious way, and I sometimes do the same – quietly watching for signs of goodness, sneaking up on it, hoping to see it clearly in all its ordinariness and splendor. I know there's a significant overpopulation of deer, making them fairly easy to spot during hunting season, but surely goodness teems and overflows far more than deer, enabling me, if I'm sincerely stalking it, to catch sight of it everywhere. This world of ours is a goodness hunter's paradise. There's goodness in every face I see, every smile, every glance between friends, every hand offering help. There's goodness, somehow or other, in every house, every car, every store, down every street. I sometimes set out on a lighthearted hunt, knowing I'll have success within a few minutes, maybe just across the street where birds are bringing sticks to a new nest. That's goodness, and it's given to all of us to hunt and be happy with, no weapons needed.

※ ※

## ANOTHER KIND OF TOUGHNESS

In my experience, a lot of guys get satisfaction from saying something like "I CAN do this, man!" It might be "I CAN lift this 100 pound weight!", or "I CAN climb this mountain!" or "I CAN do the Boston Marathon in my wheelchair!" However, I don't recall hearing a guy shout something like "I CAN accept failure!" or "I CAN handle being hurt!" Many males of my generation grew up with the idea that toughness meant always defeating something – overcoming a towering obstacle, or beating incredible odds, or crushing some enemy or other. Life was a battle, we were taught, and better to take the winner's ribbon than the loser's shame. Luckily, I've slowly learned a different definition of male toughness. I've seen that there can be as much heroism in defeat as in victory, as much gallantry in welcoming and learning from loss as in taking pride in triumph. Growing up, I was taught that being vulnerable was a sign of male weakness, but now I see that there's bravery in staying open to being hurt, in allowing myself to live, and learn from, a full life, complete with big wins and ruinous losses. Guys who accept vulnerability with poise are prepared for a gallant kind of victory. Men who can make honest failure a badge to wear and a teacher to learn from have the truest kind of toughness.

※ ※

## EASING UP

I'm easing up these days, partly because I'm starting to understand a significant fact about life. I grew up with the belief that the nature of reality was what might be called "many-ness", but now I see that it's much closer to oneness. From my earliest memory, it was impressed upon me (by family, friends, the media, and the overall culture) that life consists of many different people, many different situations, and many different ideas, all of which are struggling with each other. Life, as I learned it growing up, was a continuous conflict among innumerable elements. My main responsibility, I learned, was to save myself from harm and try to triumph in as many of the daily contests as possible. Now, however, in my eighth decade of trying to figure things out, I've come to understand that the manyness approach to reality is simply wrong. Instead of being many, the Universe is *just one*. It's not a confused collection of disparate material entities, but rather a single, cohesive, and harmonious expression of itself. The entire Universe, I see now, is as unified as a single cell. As in a cell, everything that happens in the Universe happens for the good of itself. What this means for me is that I should give up stressing and struggling, because there's no other person or other thing that's out to hurt "me". In fact, *there's no "other" at all, and no separate "me"*. There's just the one shared and always successful Universe, of which I and everyone and all of our so-called problems are a part. We're all part of a single impressive enterprise called Life (of which death is also part), as closely interlaced with each other as the insides of a cell. This realization, to me, calls for a lot more loosening up in life than struggling.

―✦ ✦―

## IDOLS

If an idol can be defined as an image or representation of a god used as an object of worship, then some of us, myself included, are occasional idol worshippers. Do we, for instance, sometimes worship the weather as though it were a god? Do we say to approaching storms, "O storm, you have so much power. Please spare me and my family!" Do we, in a sense, kneel before the storm's power, putting ourselves in the position of supplicants beseeching the storm for clemency, as though the storm is far more powerful than our small, helpless selves? And what about illness? Haven't some of us, myself included, bowed before an illness, as if it were a golden idol or a statue in a sanctuary, as if it somehow ruled our lives and just might, if entreated, treat us lightly and leave us alone? I guess I'm tired of worshipping these idols. They are not gods, and their power can't come close to matching the power all of us have in our hearts – the power of courage and calmness and perseverance. I hope I can refuse to drop to my knees in front of future storms or diseases. I hope I can say to them, "You want to see real power? Just look inside my mind and heart!"

# IN GOOD HANDS

L ike most of us, I have spent a significant amount of time concerned about my safety and security, but sometimes it comes to
me with clarity that this infinite and friendly universe has me in
its very good hands. The truth is that I am not a separate, solitary
person, but an essential and sheltered part of a single everlasting
force, sometimes called God, the Tao, or just the Universe – a force
that is always doing what is absolutely perfect for itself. If I close my
eyes, I can see my life as a waft in a wind that never started and will
never stop, or a wave in an endless ocean. How can this waft or this
wave possibly be harmed? They can change, certainly – every atom
in this universe is constantly transforming – but instead of fearing
these changes, I should try to appreciate them. This astonishing
universe takes good care of uncountable atoms and cells and particles, forever and ever, and it will take good care of that part of
itself called "Hamilton Salsich".

## YO-YOING AT FACULTY MEETINGS

I occasionally do a few tricks with my old yo-yo, and I sometimes feel like doing it during faculty meetings, especially those in which we pass judgment and set labels on students. I'm fairly good at yo-yoing, but I have *no* skill in judging and pigeonholing people. Who am I, for heaven's sake, to presume that I can analyze, classify, and label another human being? You may as well ask me to analyze the movements of the stars or paste a label on a cyclone. I know what my students *do*, but I have no idea why they do it. I can be fairly competent in *describing* student behavior, but not in branding that behavior, giving it a name, putting it in a category, placing an identifying sticker on it. It's hard for me to sit in these meetings and pretend that I understand the inner-lives of kids who are as multifaceted as the solar system. Something I do understand is how yo-yos work, and soon my colleagues may see me rise from my seat and begin doing rock-the-cradles.

⊨⧏ ⧐⊨

## IN THE BEGINNING

I've usually been befuddled by the Bible's assertion that "in the beginning was the Word", but lately I've been seeing some significance in the phrase. Words are, in a sense, one of the foremost starting points of creation in our lives. Words are thoughts made into shapes and sounds, and thoughts are a central source of power for us. Our thoughts, moment by moment, mold our experience, and our thoughts take form as spoken or written words, which stream through our lives like productive winds and sunshine. In all of human history, hasn't every disagreement, including all-out war, started with contentious words? And hasn't every single friendship started with the speaking or writing of gracious words? Words work their magic on a moment to moment basis – the magic of malice or the magic of compassion and devotion. In the beginning of both hatred and love there was, and still is, the word – a single word or a series of these irresistible written or spoken forces.

＝◆＋◆＝

## SEEING MORE CLEARLY

When things seem stirred up in my life, sometimes all I have to do is see more clearly. I've found that if I can simply notice the usually unnoticed things around me, life feels lighter and more leisurely. If, for instance, I take some time to tour my wife's garden on an abundant day in May and actually see the assorted shades of the blossoms, actually notice the slight shifting of the flowers in the faintest winds, I almost always come away with a quieter feeling about life. Problems seem simpler after I've studied the colors of clouds for a few seconds, or seen the different ways two houses shine in the sunlight, or observed the movement among millions of leaves in windy trees. Even taking the time to notice the patterns in one of my wife's colorful table cloths, or the way a window shows the shades of early morning light, might make a day seem so effortless, its potential problems so powerless and easy to solve.

＝◆＋◆＝

## INFINITE POSSIBILITIES

It sometimes seems awe-inspiring to me how many possibilities exist in my life – how many different thoughts, feelings, and events could possibly happen, even in the next few moments. It's like I'm a small stream in an endless ocean of possibilities. Who knows what will happen in the next few hours, or even the next few seconds – what current of life will come and carry me along, what thoughts will waft me here and there, what surprises will suddenly show themselves? The verb "to surprise" originally meant "to seize", and it does sometimes seem like I'm seized, moment by moment, by one startling surprise after another. True, I don't often think about this aspect of life – this tendency of life to be reborn and brand-new each moment – but it's there, nonetheless. Each second, the shoreless ocean of my life shifts, a little or a lot, and a new and splendid surprise appears.

## INFINITE TREASURES

As I was looking at some of our bookshelves from across the room yesterday, they seemed like shelves of treasures – rows and rows of riches past measuring. Each book seemed like a separate precious item, like a little chest that chose us to find its fortune. These are books we've had for years, but only yesterday did they appear to throw off, all of them, the kind of light really great books can give. I realized, maybe for the first time, that each of these books contains countless ideas and feelings – that I could search a single Shakespeare play for days and even years and not know the limits of its wisdom. The way each of these books works is the way a limitless gold mine works: you walk in and start searching and don't stop because it doesn't end. I might live for twenty more years, but it would take ten times twenty years to take in all the treasures of these books – these small, simple-looking packages of paper and print on the shelves beside our fireplace.

## IT IS GOOD FOR ME TO BE HERE

In a story in the Bible, some friends experience a special moment, one that transforms their lives into something astonishing and even sacred, and they all say, "It is good for us to be here" – and I'm trying to say the same thing many times each day. Indeed, it is *always* good for me to be wherever I am, even if the circumstances seem utterly unlucky. Any situation, no matter how cheerless, has secret payoffs, if I can stay right where I am with patience and curiosity. Instead of shunning burdensome situations, I need to stand strong and interested in the midst of them. I should prepare picnics for misfortune and fearfulness when they occasionally come by, should make them comfortable so they can teach me something. When mishaps and trials show up, as they will, I need to say, "It is good for me to be here with you. What are your lessons for today?"

＝✛ ✛＝

## IT WAS VERY GOOD

Recently, as people were leaving a family celebration, I heard someone say the party was "very good", and I said to myself, "Yes indeed, and so is everything else." I've thought a lot about that over the last few years, because finding something good in everything has slowly become a fundamental goal in my life. It's not an easy task, not with so much sorrow in the world, not with misfortunes and disasters seemingly everywhere – but still, it's a search I'm set on pursuing. I want to uncover goodness even where sadness seems most devastating. I want to see the kindness that's created right where wickedness has done its worst. This is essentially a first-class universe I'm living in, a place designed far more for success than disappointment, and I'm looking for the successes even inside the disappointments. I've seen my share of sorrow, and sometimes it's been hard to see the secret victories concealed beneath it. Where there's heartbreak, it's hard to talk of hope; where gloominess comes, as it does to all of us, liking your life seems a distant daydream. However, I continue to be convinced that thoughtfulness and goodwill will give me a new start after every setback. I continue to search for the seeds of goodness that can push up through the weeds of unhappiness. When things seem bad, compassion is still ready to give me its best. Seeing the goodness sometimes requires a serious search, but for me it's a stirring and satisfying one.

⊷ ⊶

## JUST BEGINNING

"She said she was just beginning to understand her selfishness."

-- Sarah Orne Jewett, in "Miss Sydney's Flowers"

I don't think I'm any more selfish than the next person, but strangely enough, like Miss Sydney in Jewett's story, I seem to be just starting to understand my particular type of selfishness. I'm not an unusually greedy person, and I do show a reasonable concern for others, so I don't think my personal kind of selfishness is especially spiteful. No, what I'm beginning to see is that I am selfish simply because I'm consumed with concern about my "self", the supposedly separate person I call "me". I'm starting to appreciate the fact that most of my thoughts have been about this "self", hoping to either protect it or enhance it or use it to stand strong against others. Somehow, over the years, I've nourished the notion that nothing is more important than shielding and strengthening this small, separate self called "me" -- and now, in my 70's, I'm just starting to understand how irrepressible this preoccupation has become. This, to me, is selfishness of a high order, and it's something I want to hold up in a light, look at clearly, and then hopefully leave behind. This meager and insignificant "me" which has occupied so much of my time for 71 years must be set on the scrap pile where it belongs. The only "self" I want to support and make stronger in my senior-citizen years is the one called "the world", the vast, mysterious marvel of which each of us is an indissoluble part. That would be a commitment, a dedication, worth undertaking, far more praiseworthy than the pledge to protect a silly little "me".

⊫⧾ ⧾⊨

## JUST BENEATH EVERYTHING

I'm slowly learning that if I look under old or unlucky things, I can almost always find windfalls waiting for me, though I still rarely remember to look. If I feel frayed and worn in my 70's, I can lift up that feeling and there's the sparkle that's always been there, bringing brand new life to me moment by moment. If something crashes in my life, I can look beneath the debris to discover the wisdom that waits there in its surprisingly shining wrapping. Something beneficial always reveals itself if I simply remember to lift up what looks frightful and find it there, just where it always is, where good gifts always are, just beneath everything.

⊫⧾ ⧾⊨

# JUST SITTING

Delycia and I sometimes sit in the sunroom in a silent sort of way, just enjoying the pleasures of staying still for a few moments, and often it starts me thinking about other things that are sitting still. Stones, for instance, trillions of them across the earth, are sitting close to where they've been sitting for possibly hundreds or thousands of years, staying put just as we do in our sunroom, silent and steady. It's as if stones see more good sense in just sitting than in rushing around. If they were alive, I'd say stones are wise enough to find peace precisely where they are. Delycia and I are not stones, but we do sometimes sit like them in the sunroom. It's a good way to wait for a feeling of appreciation and restfulness to come our way, and usually, within a few minutes, it does.

━━◦┼ ┼◦━━

## WHAT IS LIFE?
The most important question anyone needs to answer is "What is life?" – and I am lucky enough to gradually be learning the answer.

First, I'm learning what life is *not*. It's not anything connected to matter -- not our bodies or big cars or vacations or varieties of things we can purchase and own. Stated differently, life is not what I always thought it was, a force that somehow resides in and arises out of material objects, like human bodies. Life, I'm slowly seeing, is actually the direct opposite of matter. It's the limitless force that comes from *thoughts* instead of things – the mental, or spiritual, energy that's at work in its calm and compelling way for all the 80,000+ moments in every 24-hour day. Wherever I am today, whatever situation I may find myself in, my "life" will always be what it always is -- a constant current of thoughts, conceptions, awarenesses. It will be something like a river – say the Mississippi, that wide and deep waterway that has ceaselessly streamed through the Midwest for centuries. At 9:31 am today, or 2:14 pm, or 9:03 pm, "life" will have nothing to do, really, with anything made of matter, but instead will simply be this ever-present river of mental currents. At any given moment, all the energy I feel will be the direct result of the irrepressible flow of thoughts, a force I'll be flowing with and learning from forever.

⊷┼ ┼⊶

## KEEPERS

As we were driving one morning on wide, well-marked country roads, I thought of the anonymous workers who keep things safe and efficient for the rest of us. I call them "the keepers", those unknown laborers who let us live secure and useful lives by keeping roads and power lines and sewers working smoothly. Delycia and I lead relatively unruffled lives, partly because various keepers keep doing their mostly invisible jobs. Because the keepers of the roads we ride on work steadily and skillfully, the roads, when we need them, seem smooth and sometimes almost new. The keepers of power lines labor in storms and darkness so our homes have power whenever we need it, and the keepers of the unseen sewers below us dependably do their indispensable part to help our communities stay clean. All these keepers do their work almost entirely unnoticed and unappreciated. Their largely disregarded efforts mean Delycia and I can live lives of – compared to most of the world – astonishing ease. I'm indebted to these steadfast keepers. Perhaps I should thank one sometime.

⊨⧾ ⧾⊨

## LIKING WITHOUT KNOWING

"It was not absolutely necessary to know her in order to like her."

-- Charlotte Bronte, in *Shirley*

We often say that we need to "get to know" someone in order to really like them, but reading Charlotte Bronte's sentence this morning started me thinking in a different direction. Isn't it possible to see a smiling face and instantly like the person? We certainly wouldn't *love* the person immediately, but we can surely like the look of friendliness, and therefore sincerely like the person, if only in a kind of casual way. Similarly, I can see people who look lighthearted and uplifted, and I can quickly like them without wondering if I should first get to know them. After all, I like sunsets without knowing anything scientific about them, and I like the look of morning light on flowers, despite knowing next to nothing about the nature of light or flowers. I guess I'm talking about a sort of instantaneous liking, like suddenly seeing sheets of stars across the sky and simply feeling lucky to be seeing them, and liking both the feeling and the stars.

⊨⧾ ⧾⊨

## LAUGHING AT SELFISHNESS

I sometimes have a good laugh at my almost constant attitude of self-centeredness. I don't mean that I'm an especially selfish person, just that most of the moments of my days seem to be centered around a small, separate self called "me". I seem to see life as a series of events featuring this separate self, called "me", who is set against zillions of other separate "selves", living and non-living, each struggling to stay safe. It's as if the universe is a novel, and this small "me" in Mystic, Connecticut, is one of the main characters. Even as I wrote that sentence, the laughableness, the absolute absurdity of it, was obvious. The universe is not a novel, but a boundless and inscrutable mystery, and I am a mere wisp somewhere in the vastness of it all. Seeing myself as separate and special is like seeing a passing breeze as a small, disconnected, self-governing draft of air. As I laugh at this foolish self-centeredness, I laugh with the deepest thankfulness, for I feel fortunate that the universe is *not* made of separate selves, but is a smooth-working, harmonious whole. It thrills me to know that I and all of us are small but essential dancers in a dance that never starts and never ends. It makes me laugh to think that I could ever be misled into something as naive and inane as self-centeredness.

⊷⊶

## SIGNS AND WONDERS

I saw some "signs and wonders" this morning, things that made my world seem fairly miraculous. They were the most commonplace things – the water that flowed from the faucet as soon as I turned the handle, the simple J.C. Penney socks I slipped on that seemed made to perfection, the toaster that popped up perfectly-prepared raisin toast. Sometimes, miracles seem to be everywhere. Thoughts, for instance, miraculously materialize in my mind, moment after moment, many thousands in a day, all seeming to sail in from nowhere. And my lungs, amazingly, have reliably lifted and fallen approximately 750,000,000 times in my lifetime, and are effortlessly doing it as I write this. Even the sunlight, which is now shining through our southern windows, is a wonder, a sign of the absolute charm of the universe, and of my life. Each day, one way or another, sunlight lights up my world – a daily marvel, a miracle among the many that seem to surround me.

## LAZY DAYS

I know my hard-working, un-retired friends may find this annoying, but I have to say it anyway: I sometimes enjoy the laziest of days. When I was teaching, I loved my work, and in retirement I sometimes love my idleness. I can be positively work-shy, and love it. I can happily loll, loaf, and loiter through most of a day. I have tons of time on my hands each day, and I can happily kill it all. In my 70's, I can be a totally shiftless dude, as though I'm riding in a slow-moving, old-fashioned, going-nowhere horse-drawn buggy. I can be completely remiss in my duties to the dishes and the dusting rag. I can basically bum around from breakfast on, lollygagging and twiddling my thumbs. I can be slack, lax, and lackadaisical – just taking a break after 45 years of teaching. No, I don't intend to fritter away *all* my senior days, but I'm "as old as the hills", and some days I am pleased to be as idle and undisturbed as the oldest of them.

## A LOVING RAMBLE

Lately I've noticed leaves falling from trees in a most undisturbed and slow-moving manner, just one every few seconds, sidling slowly down in their own sweet time. We haven't yet reached the days when there's a daily downpour of leaves, and so we have these single leaves that seem to linger in the air as they waft their way here and there above the lawns and streets. Watching them for a few minutes this morning, I thought of some people I've known who seemed able to live like these leaves, sort of floating effortlessly with the updrafts and downdrafts of life. They seemed to instinctively know that nothing is gained by grappling with life, and that a good way to live is to let life lead the way in its whimsical manner. These people worked hard, yes, and they reliably did their duties, but I always saw a smoothness in their actions, almost as though they were amusing themselves rather than working. Like the solitary leaves that glide above us with ease in these early autumn days, these friends from my past made living look like a loving ramble rather than a demanding ordeal.

# LEAVENING THE WORLD

"… Arthur […] leavened the world."

- Alfred Tennyson, *The Idylls of the King*

The poet Tennyson tells us that King Arthur constantly "leavened the world", a beautiful way of describing how a person can help everything around him rise up with refreshing power. Like yeast does to bread dough, Arthur's goodwill gave life to his kingdom, and perhaps, in small ways, I can enliven the little realm in which I live. Arthur suffused those around him with both courage and graciousness, and maybe, in my small ways, I can do something similar. By instilling my words and actions with both confidence and courtesy, perhaps I can ever so slightly lift the lives of others. Maybe, by living in a thankful way, I can make those around me more aware of the gifts given to all of us each moment. I'm no king, just an old, grateful guy who wants to give back, and a way to do it might be to quietly permeate everything around me with the lightheartedness I'm lucky to have. Like leaven, even a little cordiality and hopefulness can lighten and lift up almost any life.

━━◁┼ ┼▷━━

## A GENTLE BUT BRAVE HAND

The word "tact" takes its meaning from the Latin word for "touch", suggesting that tactful people touch the world around them with care and consideration. They connect with things and people and situations in an understanding way. They *stroke* life, self-assuredly brushing it with their thoughts and words and actions, instead of shoving or striking it. Whatever they come into contact with – their work, other people, the weather, illness, disaster – they do it with sensitivity, *savoir faire,* and gallantry. Being tactful, they hold out a gentle but brave hand to everything.

━━◁┼ ┼▷━━

## LEAVES LETTING GO

I wonder if I could conduct myself more often the way the autumn leaves are living in these last days of their lives. To use a familiar phrase, they're simply "letting go", setting themselves loose from their limbs and allowing the breezes to bring them where they will. They're surrendering, in a sense, submitting to the stronger powers of winds and seasons, and in that surrender, I see a kind of lighthearted liberty. I know they're just leaves, but perhaps people like me could learn from them – learn to allow more than resist, to let go more than grasp and cling. The winds will take the leaves where they need to go, and maybe my days, if I trust them, will deliver me, each evening, to exactly where I'm best prepared to be.

Leaves seem to sense when it's time to float instead of hold tight, a lesson I may be just starting to learn.

━◁+ +▷━

## LETTING

"Let" is a little word I want to work into my life more often. I want, for instance, to sometimes let things happen the way they seem to want to happen, instead of always insisting on the way I want them to happen. I want to let life flow along like the infinite river it is, instead of setting up endless barriers and re-routings so it will do what I want it to do. I want to even let hard luck or heartbreak happen, as they sometimes inescapably will, and then let my endless inner spirit spread out to welcome and accommodate and learn from them.

━◁+ +▷━

# LIGHTHEARTED LIVING

L iving in a light-hearted way would be a good goal for me. To have a heart – an inner spirit, a mindset – as light as the summer winds that are wandering among my wife's unfolding flowers this morning would be something special. There's too much heaviness in the world – too many burdens brought on by our countless cares and concerns – and I'd like to lesson the load. I'd like to set down my personal pack and dance a little. I'd like to learn from the lightness that's all around me – from the sunlight that always floats and never forces or pushes, from the breezes that seem as carefree as hopeful thoughts, from the occasional single clouds that hover above us as if they're satisfied with the way things are. There's bending under burdens, and then there's sailing with buoyancy and spirit – and I now choose the latter.

―――+――

### LIKE A LION ROARING
Sometimes I see things so startling that it's almost like a lion roaring to remind me of how surprising life is. These wake-up

calls come not from strange and outlandish things, but from just the simplest, most commonplace stuff of everyday life. If I'm sort of dozing in my thoughts while walking around the yard, suddenly I might see a set of trees along our street standing so straight and self-possessed, and I'm startled into wakefulness by the simple rightness of them. Or, if I'm sleepwalking through some humdrum household tasks, out of the blue I might notice a yellow bowl on a table beside a window, and that small, undistinguished bowl seems to shout at me to wake up and watch for the ever-present wonders around me. These lions in my life, thank heavens, roar quite regularly to keep me alert. I can effortlessly daydream through most of any day, but usually some small, obvious thing – a single shadow on the lawn, a fluttering leaf, a sky so blue it stuns – roars to me now and then, and I bow in my heart in thanks.

━◁+ +▷━

## A FORCE TO RELY ON

I guess all of us wish we could find, some way or another, a force that we can always rely on, a force that's always present for us and that can't be conquered – and I think I've found one. Friendliness, it seems to me, is as present for us as the sky, and just as immeasurable and impregnable. After all, what problem can overpower our ability to be pleasant, to show some fellowship, to support and smile and say something that lifts instead of disheartens? Can't friendliness survive even cancer, even a crushing kind of sorrow? In the midst of terror or tornadoes, can't outgoingness and cordiality stay strong, and even grow stronger? It makes me think, surprisingly, of the simplest of math formulas. In the worst disaster, in sadness that strikes straight to the heart, in a failure that seems to foretell the failure of everything, *2+2 is still 4*, and friendliness is still full of almighty force. If winds work havoc and lightning burns my personal world away,

2+2 would still be 4, and friendliness, vast and everlasting, would still stand strong and tall.

⊷

## LIVING LIKE AN ESSAY

For many years I made my students write essays, but only recently have I thought about the possibility of *living* like an essay. The French verb "essayer" means "try or attempt", and perhaps it can be loosely translated as "take a chance, experiment, see what happens next." Michel de Montaigne, known as the western world's first essayist, took a chance with his writing. His sentences and paragraphs were experiments in sincere, unrestrained thinking. He let his words loose on the page to see what would happen next, and thereby gave future writers (including my students) a new and powerful way to write with both honesty and zest. I wonder if a person could *live* that way – I mean live like an essay, like a moment-by-moment experiment to see what would happen next? Could a 73-year-old guy like me set aside his plans and projects and strategies and wariness and worries, and just let the experiment called life take place? Could he let the river of each day flow freely, like the words of a good essay, each fearless sentence leading easily to the next, each unmatched moment making ready for the next?

⊷

## LOADED WITH GOOD LIFE

This morning I noticed Delycia's tall sunflowers all folded over and drooping down with the weight of their seeds, and they seemed, as I studied them, to represent the loads of good life that lean down on all things these early autumn days. Many lawns, for instance, seem well-stocked with healthful grass, and trees are loaded with the luxury of leaves and seeds. Often, as was true yesterday, the sky seems laden with puffed-up clouds, and even the slice of the moon these nights might seem unusually overloaded with light. It's true for me, also, although I sometimes don't notice it – don't notice the goodness this world is full of, don't feel the overflow of kindheartedness and courage all around me, don't see the spilling over of startling occurrences, second by second. Just now a tufted titmouse twirled in the air near the feeder for a few seconds, a small, full bundle of spinning feathers, just one sample of the miracles that make autumn – and sunflowers – almost sag with prosperity and splendor.

## LOOKING AT LILIES

Yesterday, as I was looking carefully at some of the pearly, pristine blossoms of Delycia's asiatic lilies, I felt a blossoming feeling of reassurance. In this seemingly self-destructive world, where countless children are any war's victims and where chaos and abhorrence sometimes seem far more prevalent than contentment and comradeship, it's cheering to stand before the simple loveliness of a single lily blossom. Looking at lilies, really looking at them and seeing their implausible charm, one feels an unfolding of hope inside. Yes, there seems to be dislike and disorder everywhere, but look for lilies, too. Beauty of far greater power than evil is all around us, even in a small garden in a small seaside town.

## LOSING AND FINDING

After losing my keys yesterday and then finding them fairly quickly, I started thinking about how frequently I find things – sometimes surprising things in surprising places. I once found a dozen silver dollars on an old blanket on the beach. There they sat, bright and unblemished in the sunlight, with scarcely a person to be seen anywhere. I stared at them for a moment and then moved on, feeling lucky to have found them and then left them where they were. Likewise, I feel lucky, when I'm writing, to almost always find useful and sometimes startling words waiting for me in my word processor's thesaurus. It's as though thousands upon thousands of words are standing by to bring stylishness to my writing, poised to present themselves inside my sentences with their glow and gracefulness. I've sometimes found a word that, by itself, instantly added finesse to an otherwise plain paragraph. It's true for thoughts, too, for they can be found in unforeseen ways and places, as though they're hidden riches that ascend to the surface occasionally. For no reason that I can understand, thoughts arise inside me by the millions, some with an enticing shine, and, to my satisfaction, I get to sort through them and select the brightest and best for my writing. It's like finding diamonds day after day, which should be a pleasing project for these chock-full and comforting retirement years.

⟞⟝⟞⟝

## MEEKNESS

A famous man once said that meekness in a person is a blessed thing, and I think I'm finally starting to see his meaning. It now seems clear to me that meekness can be a strength instead of a deficiency. In meekness, surprisingly, we sometimes stand up stronger than in assertiveness. When we surrender, we sometimes win. Trees that survive are those that submit to strong winds instead of resisting them, and water almost always wins because it yields itself softly to obstructions. Meekness means a brave kind of obedience. Streams are obedient to boulders and thus flow effortlessly around them. Flowers are obedient to breezes and bow with ease and elegance. I am obedient to my heart and lungs and let them lead the way. In meekness we are mild in a daring way, gentle in just the way the strongest trees are.

━┼─ ─┼━

## SQUIRREL MIGHT

When I was in elementary school, we sometimes had tugs-of-war at recess, and I recall older kids calling out, "Pull with all your might!" They meant "might" like in human muscles and strong-mindedness, but I've been noticing a simpler, more commonplace example of might, right in our backyard. It's the might, the sheer single-mindedness, of the squirrels that spring up several feet to find a footing on one of the bird feeders. They usually slip and slide and quickly crash down again, but they're always back at it with stubbornness fairly soon. Back in 4th grade, we pulled on the rope with all our might, but these squirrels seem to *live* with all their might. Whether leaping across the lawn, or scrambling for seeds that have fallen from the feeder, or dashing up the sides of trees sometimes to their summits and then swaying with the wind, the squirrels at 44 Riverbend Drive do their living with a kind of might that can make a sometimes sluggish senior citizen envious.

━┼─ ─┼━

## MIRACLE MEALS

It occurs to me that, at the mediation center where we recently participated in a retreat, many people made their meals a sort of meditation, but that my meals at home, for the most part, are the opposite – a sort of unseeing sprint through food in order to find the next thing I need to do. It's more like dashing than eating, more like three-times-a-day madness than mindfulness. Being in the stillness and repose of the meditation center, and eating among people who patiently took pleasure in their meals, has raised in me the desire to switch to a slower, more mellow kind of eating. I want to relish the look of linguine before I taste it, and take pleasure in the aromas arising from a full bowl of soup. I want to savor the food I eat, even the slim sandwich at lunch, even the small slice of tomato in the salad. I want to chew like the food was chosen just for me, chew like love and long life will come from chewing. Eating, it seems to me, should be like thinking greatly, or singing with a full feeling of freedom, or sitting beside someone you love because you're in love. A meal done that way could be a miracle.

# MISHMASHING

When I grow bored with being organized and efficient, I sometimes settle cheerfully into the coolness and poise of disorganization. Then, I accept my disorders and mishmashes as no worse than the way leaves lie across lawns in graceful confusion in the autumn. I compare myself to clouds in the sky as they scatter and shift and reshuffle themselves in their beautifully messy way. Being neat is a nice way to live, but here's a cheer, too, for occasional clutter and even some harmless chaos. I see little orderliness on the beaches we walk, with their picturesque swirls of sand and driftwood and stones, and sometimes I let my life be like that, let the waves of life wash in and shape my minutes every which way.

---

## MOMENTIALS
Perhaps a new word is needed in our dictionaries, something like "momential", to describe things that recur moment by moment,

the way perennial flowers return year after year. My wife has complete confidence that her Japanese irises will arise and blossom each year, and we can have a similar sense of assurance about the things that start up in our lives moment after moment. For instance, I know for sure that a totally new feeling will flow into me each moment. Like the irises, the feeling may seem the same as yesterday's or last year's, but there will always be a subtle uniqueness in the feeling of each moment, similar to the slight and special differences in each year's irises. Feelings, you might say, are "momential" because new ones arise in their abundance and freshness moment after moment. Even the breaths we take are newly born second by second, sending fresh life to our cells. The irises return each summer, and the gentle work of oxygen generates just what our bodies need in the next new moment. Like the flowers that unfold for us perennially, our lungs dependably lift and fall momentially -- moment after moment after moment.

⚬

## A GRAVE, PENETRATING KINDNESS

"[Maggie] saw it was Dr. Kenn's face that was looking at her; that plain, middle-aged face, with *a grave, penetrating kindness* in it, seeming to tell of a human being who had reached a firm, safe strand, but was looking with helpful pity toward the strugglers still tossed by the waves, had an effect on Maggie at this moment which was afterward remembered by her as if it had been *a promise.* The middle-aged, who have lived through their strongest emotions, but are yet in the time when memory is still half passionate and not merely contemplative, should surely be a sort of natural priesthood, whom life has disciplined and consecrated to be the refuge and rescue of early stumblers and victims of self-despair."

-- from George Eliot's *The Mill on the Floss*

I have often been accused of excessive idealism, so my appreciation of this passage will not surprise my friends. I entirely agree with what Eliot suggests about the role older people, including older teachers, can play. I took pleasure in the fact that, in my last years as a teacher, in my 60's and early 70's, I could show "a grave, penetrating kindness" toward my students. At that point in my life, it was not a silly, irresponsible kindness, one that simply wanted to win over the students and become their "friend", but rather a kindness that had some weightiness behind it and could sometimes penetrate into the heart of a situation. It was a kindness, I might say, that wore work gloves instead of kid gloves, a kindness that delivered itself to the students more like strong medicine than a sugary soft drink. In Eliot's words, I felt like I had, in some sense, "reached a firm, safe strand", from where I could offer a helping hand to the "strugglers", my sometimes befuddled but brave teenage students. Having lived 50+ more years than they, I had "been there, done that" so often that I could, to some degree, show the way to the wandering souls in my classes. Perhaps, as the author suggests, older teachers can stand before their students like a "promise" – a guarantee that the darkness can eventually become a little lighter. She uses the words "natural priesthood", which might smack of egotism and false pride, but there may be some truth in the idea that a senior teacher can fulfill the role of a "priest", who, to use the original Greek definition, could be thought of as simply an "elder", someone who's been through the wars, survived, and returned to offer instructions and warnings.

And after all, don't these young people in our classrooms need that? Don't they need to hear, in the midst of the mayhem and dread of these times, words from the enduring veterans of life's wars, words that carry gravity, kindness, and a promise?

❧ ☙

## MY ANGELS

For Christians and others, Christmas is the season of angels, but I've been realizing in the last few years that angels visit me almost every minute of the day. The word "angel", after all, simply means "messenger" (from the Greek "angelos"), and what better messengers are there than the thoughts that arrive at my life each day?

❧ ☙

## A BEST FRIEND

If we say a best friend is one who is always faithful, then, strange as it seems, the present moment is one of my best friends. Being always by my side – *always*, no matter how bad things get – the present moment is unswerving in its promise to me. In the sunshine of bliss or the darkness of sorrow, the present moment is right there with me, as new as a new day. It's the most steadfast of friends, and, more importantly, the most perfect of friends, since it is always exactly what it has to be. Something is perfect if it is as good as it is possible for it to be, which means this present moment (and the next one, and the next) is, indeed, perfect. I can make the *next* moment be different, but this exact moment, right now, is superbly what it must be. What luck, to have a faithful and perfect friend with me, moment by moment!

❧ ☙

## MY BEST

Like most of us, I have been trying to "do my best" for most of life, but lately I've been looking at another way of living – a different sense, you might say, of what doing my best might mean. As I was making a start on this paragraph this morning, I caught sight of some clouds that were shifting their shapes in the sky outside the window by my desk, and it occurred to me that they were the best clouds they could possibly be. They weren't struggling or striving or working out ways to be the best; they simply were, and always would be, as good as clouds could be. Even if they slipped off into just wispy streams of whiteness, they would be the best possible wispy streams of whiteness. I thought of this as I sat at my computer in my crumpled shirt and wrinkled pants, and it seemed like I was similar to those clouds, and maybe just as marvelous as they always are. Maybe I don't need to struggle so sincerely to be the best I can be, because perhaps, in a sense, I always am. Maybe my saggy shirt sags in the best ways possible, and maybe the dirt on my pants is perfectly placed and displays the best possible shades of brown. If I can't seem to think of the finest words for this paragraph, perhaps, like those always perfect clouds, I can confidently come up with words that will shine with their own proper brightness. Maybe the best I can do is simply believe in who I am at this mint-condition moment, and let each word do its own remarkable work.

―≒― ―≒―

## NEVER ALONE

In my past, when suffering from different stresses and sorrows, I sometimes felt very alone, but in these senior years now, I'm slowly seeing that I can never really be alone, for I am an essential and inseparable piece of a single magnificent extravaganza called the Universe. I am surrounded at all times by "friends" who faithfully follow me and provide what I need to stay strong with all of them – the breath that brings life to my lungs each second; the outside sights and sounds that are always there for me and mix with me and become part of who I am; the thoughts that flow through me from east and west and who knows where. The same life-force that streams through me flows also through hills and homes and the littlest limbs on trees. We are all together, as one, in this cohesive river called life. The atoms in my body are billions of years old, and have once been in sheep or soil or far-off stars. Perhaps the oxygen I just breathed in was part of persons in Slovakia or Senegal yesterday, making them my distant but very necessary friends. No, I couldn't possibly be alone even if I wanted to. Togetherness and Fellowship are other names for this spectacle we sometimes call God, and sometimes the Universe.

## NO SEPARATE ENDS

"O mountain friends!
With mine your solemn spirit blends,
And life no more hath separate ends."

-- John Greenleaf Whittier, "Lake Winnipesaukee"

Since I often feel like I'm seeking separate objectives from everyone else, as if my goals, or ends, were given to me alone and I must make my way toward them on my own, it was wonderful to come upon these words of Whittier yesterday. On the shores of Lake Winnipesaukee, the poet came to understand the truth that, in fact, there are no "separate ends" anywhere – that all of us who share this universe also share the same goals. We are all seeking, every second, a stronger sense of being simply what or who we are.

All of us – all people, animals, winds, and stars – are steering, in our special ways, toward being the best possible people, animals, winds, and stars. All of us are looking for light in a sometimes dark world, for comfort where comfort often seems far distant. I can pretend that my goals are solely mine, but that's a pretense that surely diminishes me. The truth is, as Whittier discovered beside the lake, that not one of us strives separately from others – that all of us who share this impressively mystifying universe strive step by step in a sometimes unseen but everlasting togetherness.

⊷ ⊶

## TRAUMA ON THE DANCE FLOOR

Last Friday, Delycia and I attended our first "practice dance" at the Fred Astaire Studio in Mystic (CT), and it was a tense and almost traumatic experience for me. I do love dancing with Delycia, and I definitely feel like I'm slowly learning the basic steps and movements, but Friday night I felt like I was suffering through 9th grade math class again. I seemed to have no idea how to do what was being asked of me, just as I usually felt in math class. Strobe lights were shaking across the dance floor, the music seemed to be shouting, and, for some reason, I suddenly lost everything I had learned in our dance lessons. The basic box step seemed impossible, and the swing steps caused me to stumble against my graceful partner again and again. Every so often, our instructor rushed up excitedly and asked how I was doing, and I'm sure my smile was colorless and scared-looking as I said, "Just fine", which is what I always said when my math teacher asked the same question. It was a strained and anxious few hours for me, except, thankfully, for the occasional slow dances, when I simply snuggled as close as possible to Delycia and we became two kids just coming together in love.

⊷ ⊶

# THE LITTLE TOWN INSIDE

At the Christmas season, "O Little Town of Bethlehem" is a much-loved song, and this morning it made me think about a "little town" I have inside me. In the song, the town is described as being "still" and "silent" as it waited to receive the good news of the birth of Jesus, and I sometimes have to be still and silent as I await the arrival of feelings like hopefulness and confidence. When, as happens occasionally to most of us, my life seems dark like the skies over Bethlehem, I sometimes have to simply sit in stillness, waiting for a light to shine somewhere inside, like a star over a stable. Not much good news is given in the midst of clamor and uproar, but if I can settle myself into a sort of hushed state of readiness, like little Bethlehem in the song, I usually see something fresh enter my life – something like a new birth, something like the beginning, again, of understanding and reassurance and serenity.

## OFFSPRINGING

In our blended family, Delycia and I have five children and four grandchildren – our "offspring", to use an old-fashioned word – but I've been thinking this morning about another kind of offspring we might lay claim to – our thoughts and spoken words. After all, we, in a sense, "give birth" to thoughts and words all day long, sending them out into the world as the creations – the "children" – of our minds. Each day, thousands of newborn thoughts are brought forth in our minds, and, somewhat like children, they instantly start making their presence felt. They mix with other thoughts, making more new thoughts, and then perhaps new spoken words to be newly delivered to the world. Just in the last few days, we have given birth to thousands of these full-of-life thoughts and words, these short-lived offspring that materialize in innocence and wholesomeness and help us share our lives with each other and the world.

◄═┼ ┼═►

## OLD AND NEW

Last night, we attended the opening concert at Tanglewood by the Boston Symphony Orchestra, and it was surely an evening for the old and the new. Most of the patrons were probably in their 70's and 80's, but most of them also had an easily noticeable spirit of newness. With canes and stooped shoulders, sometimes in wheel-chairs and sometimes as straight up as pillars, they showed off the strength of seniority in a stately and handsome way. These were people who had surely seen indescribable sorrows and successes in their long lives, and now, as they listened to the exquisite music of Tchaikovsky, they seemed to sit with the poise and power of their years. These were old people, yes, but they seemed somehow new and unblemished. Perhaps they felt, in some way, fulfilled, and

135

therefore full of youthfulness again. Perhaps, to them, this music of transcendent loveliness was a prize presented especially to them for sharing their strength and understanding with the world for so many years. These young-at-heart seniors essentially *made* the world we live in today, and last night the world, we might say, made music just for them.

═╬═╬═

## ONE TO ONE

Delycia and I have taken several one-to-one tutorial sessions at the Apple Store, and I've decided I could use some other similar learning sessions. One-to-one with a technology teacher can teach me much, but so, for instance, could a private class with the comforting winds that often flow through our backyard. I can see myself sitting in the shade and letting the wind whisper whatever it wants to me, perhaps teaching me a little about taking it easy and going wherever it's easiest to go. It could show me how to sometimes simply stop and be still, and then restart with ease and gracefulness. I could also sit close to our bird feeders and just be mindful of, and learn from, the charming motions of the birds during their meals. They move in a million different ways, usually fast and restlessly, but always with flawless smoothness, and I could learn from this – learn to love moving with both liveliness and gentleness, and always with composure, like the finches, who flit and flutter with assured serenity. I could just sit near the birds and stare and listen and learn, one-to-one with these fluffy and skillful teachers.

═╬═╬═

## ORDINARY DAYS

I've been thinking lately that, now in my retirement years, I'm lucky to have so many ordinary days in my life. I realize that the word "ordinary" can carry a negative connotation, suggesting monotony and tedium, but interestingly, it stems from the Latin word for "orderly", and I do love the orderly look of these senior days of mine. Confusion occasionally seems to surface, but that's usually because I'm not noticing the orderliness and rightness inside the seeming disorder. The fact is, my days are made by the universe in just the right way, perfect for me, and the many occurrences in my days are set out before me in a meticulous display, exactly in the proper pattern – if only I could see things clearly. There's an essential orderliness everywhere – in trees losing their leaves at precisely the right times, in clouds crossing the sky just as they must, even in cars cruising the roads systematically with the help of lanes and lights and signals. This universe I live in is basically an orderly miracle, and though it's not easy to see the order beneath the disarray and disasters of our times, still, my senior days, like all the days of my long life, have so far been "ordinary" in the best way – full of graceful form and structure that I'm slowly starting to see and understand.

➤← →←

## AS ONE WHO WAKES

"... as one who wakes
Half-blinded at the coming of a light."

-- Alfred Tennyson, "The Idylls of the King"

I don't ever recall waking up "half-blinded at the coming of a light", as Tennyson put it, but I do recall sometimes being so surprised by what I was seeing or reading that it was like a stunning light had been lit in my life. I've seen colors in the sky, for instance, that were startling to my eyes, and valleys of falling gray rain that seemed to shine with dusky loveliness, and even small stones on the shore that made my eyes squint at their iridescent brilliance in the sunlight. Something similar sometimes happens when I'm reading – a single word that shimmers with significance, or a phrase that seems to flash as I read it, or a sentence that throws so much light at me that I almost have to turn my eyes aside. Occasionally a whole collection of pages will sparkle intensely, as if I'm holding a bright light in my hands, and I have to set the book down and rub my eyes so I can see again.

## SEEING THE LIGHT

I've often heard people say they "see the light", meaning the meaning of something has become clear to them, and it sometimes helps me remember that a light of some sort shines in even the most commonplace parts of our lives. For instance, I can sometimes "see the light" in even the cloudiest and wettest days, meaning I can suddenly see their appropriateness, their flawlessness as excellent cloudy and wet days. I can even sometimes see the everyday special reflection of light in puddles on the pavement, a light that can make them seem strangely fascinating. This afternoon I saw the light in some sentences in a novel I was re-reading, sentences that seemed puzzling on the first reading but that lit up like lamps the second time around. Also, Delycia and I live in an undistinguished house on an unexceptional street, but there's a good light all through our lives that I'm sometimes lucky to see.

## PAIN, BUT NOT SUFFERING

In my reading recently, I came across, again, the basic Buddhist teaching that pain is inevitable but suffering is optional, and it suddenly summed up, for me, so many of the things I've been thinking about over the last 40-some years. It reminded me that there will often be pain of one sort or another in my life, but the pain can be useful instead of destructive, a friend instead of an enemy. Whatever pain I might feel in the future, whether physical or emotional, will surely be pain, but it doesn't have to be misery. It's possible to face pain the way sailors face a fierce wind at sea – by accepting its inescapability, and then welcoming its potential as a teacher, maybe even as a friend. Pain can provide the power that pushes me up to a higher level of living, where pain itself becomes less frightening and more enlightening. If I accept it and ask it to show me the way, pain can make me wiser rather than sadder, a learner instead of a sufferer.

---

## PREPARING FOR THE WEATHER (OF THE MIND)

Like most of us, I try to take appropriate preparations when serious storms are in the forecast, but I sometimes forget to get myself ready for troublesome "mental" weather. It's interesting to me that I seem more concerned about high winds and heavy snow than about devastating thoughts, and yet the thoughts can throw my life into far worse disorder than the wildest storms. Thoughts filled with fears can bring bedlam to a life faster than any blizzard, and the effects of these stormy thoughts can last a lot longer than downed wires and damaged homes. I sometimes set out flashlights and candles for coming storms, but how often do I shine the lights of optimism and poise inside my mind when I see worries working their way toward me? The scariest storm can be met with vivacity and even exuberance, and fear, frightening as it may be, can be taught a lesson about human daring simply through clear and untroubled thinking. Easy to say, hard to do, but when fear meets serenity, the latter can take the trophy -- always.

---

# PRESENCE

Perhaps all of us know people who seem to shine with what we might call "presence". These are people who seem thoroughly present, wherever they might be. When you're with them, they give the gift of being completely with you, entirely here right now. In a surprising way, the presence of these people can create in us a sense of expansiveness, almost boundlessness, as though when they enter a room the walls seem to disappear and an uncommon kind of freedom is felt. They are not only present with us, but completely pleased and satisfied to be right where they are, which sometimes makes us feel, for a few moments, something similar, something like satisfaction and reassurance and empowerment.

⇒⊱ ⊰⇐

### RACING SLOWLY, AND WITH PATIENCE

In these days of my retirement, I still do a fair amount of racing around, but I guess I'm racing around more slowly and patiently -- more willing, you might say, to good naturedly participate in the race while letting the race actually run itself. On a given day, I'm going here and there and back and forth, checking off my list of to-do's and to-get's, but now I'm running a gentler, more warmhearted race. You might say I'm *slowly* racing from task to task, and with more composure, perhaps the way sparrows seem to collect their seeds at the feeder with both quickness and calmness. I've noticed that the wind sometimes blows on our street in a similar way – rushing among the houses, but in a somehow stress-free manner, doing its to-do's with both enthusiasm and restfulness. As a senior now, I'm seeing the benefits in that kind of racing around. With my white beard and bald head, I'm breaking new records for getting things done with a cozy and easy kind of speed.

⇥ ⇤

## RAISING SHADES

This morning, when I raised the window shade in our bedroom, the daylight almost leaped into the room, something light seems to like to do. When I turn on a lamp in a dark room, the light instantly does away with the darkness, and headlights switched on can immediately transform a nighttime road with their brightness. I think, too, of the light a bright thought can instantaneously spread around my life. The sun can make my days shine, but what about the light of a single positive thought? What about the daylight a little confident thinking can quickly let into my life?

⇥ ⇤

## UNBELIEVABLE LUCK

Sometimes my good luck seems unbelievable. I'm neither wealthy nor well-known nor uncommonly gifted, but good fortune seems to follow me everywhere. I often, for instance, can't believe the simple fact that I'm alive on an astonishing planet in an implausibly beautiful universe – that somehow this person called "Ham' has been given hundreds of millions of minutes of this thing called life. The whole mystery of my life seems totally improbable, as if a magician somewhere in the everlasting cosmos made some swirls with her wand and, presto, here's Hamilton Salsich. And my incredible good fortune continues to follow me in a round-the-clock way – my heart somehow holding its rhythm 100,000 times each day, my blood reliably rolling through my body hour after hour, my lungs lifting and falling in a steadfast way. All this, to me, seems so far-fetched – so deserving of awe – that it almost requires a down-on-my-knees, lost-for-words reverence.

⊷⊶

## CHARMING CLUELESSNESS

When I was a boy, "search me" -- meaning "I have no clue" -- was a response I sometimes used when questioned about something, and I was thinking this morning that I could make it my personal slogan, since I honestly have no definite answers on almost any issue. I have occasionally enjoyed pretending I know the right answers, but the truth is, I could forage in my mind forever and still not be sure I've got the truth. All I usually find, in fact, is a formidable wilderness of possible answers, like wispy flakes moving by the millions through my mind. For me, life at 73 is almost always fun, and sometimes fantastic, but that doesn't mean I have answers. Actually, I've pretty much given up trying to find answers, and instead, I'm savoring the surprisingly charming world of my cluelessness. The sky above is immense, unsearchable, and beautiful, and so, I now see, is the universe of answers. Instead of searching, I'm just appreciating.

⊷⊶

## SEARCHING FOR ME

Unfortunately, I have spent a large part of my 72 years trying to be either defensive or aggressive – trying, that is, either to protect the so-called separate self called "me", or to launch out from that self in an active, creative way. It's been an exhausting struggle. I've had to be constantly on the alert, constantly standing by to either shield this person called "Ham" or use it as a base from which to make things happen. During most waking hours, I've been either a defender or an aggressor. Thankfully, however, things have been changing for me. The mist has slowly been dissolving. Amazingly, it's gradually becoming clear that this apparently separate, easily damaged self called "me" actually doesn't exist! This "person" I've devoted so many years to defending and empowering is actually no more than a passing thought! Whenever I search for what I call "me", all I can find is another thought. It might be a thought that I'm vulnerable and need protection, or that I'm strong and can aggressively make a mark in the world, but in either case, it's *not* a separate physical person, but simply a thought. The strange and inspiring truth seems to be that my only existence is as a fresh, free-wheeling thought in the always-new present moment. There's really no separate "Hamilton Salsich" who needs protection or who needs to feel responsible for getting a thousand things done each day. There's just the endless and shoreless river of thoughts, which some people call "God", and of which I and all of us are a part. This understanding is slowly helping me see that I can, in fact, give up being either defensive or aggressive – that I can finally loosen up, let go, and simply take pleasure in whatever happens in this capricious, always surprising universe.

⊷⊶

## ALWAYS ENOUGH

Though I'm far from being a wealthy retiree, it's reassuring to know that, barring an absolute disaster, there will always be enough resources available to supply my basic needs – and I'm not just talking about material resources. I have set aside enough money to keep myself moderately sheltered and safe, but I also have another supply of trustworthy resources – one that *can't* be exhausted. In addition to my IRAs and Social Security and scattered investments, I also have the inexhaustible endowment of inspiring thoughts. When a need arises, there will be sufficient money available, as well as – and just as important – sufficient inspiration. I will be able to access both dollars and encouraging thoughts. In fact, while I'm only modestly comfortable financially, I am, like all of us, fabulously wealthy with enriching thoughts. They overflow around me, always, and all I have to do is notice them and say "Welcome". They're a fountain of invisible resources, these everlasting affirmative thoughts that are always swift to stand me up and show me the way.

⚒ ⚒

## ON SECURITY

At the Navy submarine base in Groton, CT, where I taught an evening English class for many years, there was always a serious concern about security, which often served to remind me that the search for absolute personal security is ultimately a futile endeavor. Of course, it's important to take precautions against the possible dangers in life, but precautions will never be able to save me from all the little and large perils that are part of living a full life. Collapses and crashes and breakdowns are built into life like darkness is built into each 24-hour day, and no number of fortifications will fully protect me from all of them. The best I can do is take practical precautions day by day, and then live like I love every minute of life. When disaster comes, I hope I'll speak to it with authority, but until then, I'd rather risk it and dance with a few dangers than encircle myself with guards and barricades.

⚒ ⚒

# SEEING FREEDOM

I sometimes see, with surprising clearness, that I am freer, by far, than I ever imagined. Sometimes it becomes completely clear to me that I am not a separate, isolated, and time-bound individual, but an essential part of a freely flowing universe. The atoms that make up my mind and body were shaped at the same moment the stars started to shine and the earth to spin, and thus have sailed through billions of years with freedom, all the way to me. My thoughts, too, have sailed into my life in casual, on-the-loose ways from who knows where, and I can freely flow with those thoughts beyond all boundaries. I confess I often feel fairly bound up by all kinds of limits, but at certain special times I do know, for sure, that I'm as free as an unfettered breeze.

━┼ ┼━

## SETTLING

When I lived for a few years beside a slow-moving river, I sometimes stirred up the water in the shallows just to see it slowly settle back to its usual clearness, and occasionally, when my life seems blurred and unsettled, I still think of how, given time, that river always returned to its accustomed stillness. I guess I need to give my so-called problems, too, time to smooth down and settle. I sometimes need to do nothing but sit on the "bank" of seemingly bad situations and let them loosen and slowly resolve themselves. All too often I stir up the problems more than ever by making anxious attempts to fix things, when sitting in stillness might be a better way. Storms always, in due course, lessen and sail off in front of the sunshine, and my difficulties might do the same if not whipped up more by my fretfulness. Perhaps I should see a problem as simply a short-lived fuss and splash in the nonstop river of life, and look with confidence to see things settle and sparkle once again.

⋘ ⋙

## SHADOWS

On the windowsill of my small study, there are a few figurines of my literary heroes (Jane Austen and Charles Dickens, among others), and yesterday morning I noticed the shadows cast by the figurines on the wall by the early sunlight. Not only did I notice the shadows, but I actually studied them for a few minutes, just watching the way they shook and swayed on the wall as the leaves outside the window wavered in the breezes. There I was, sitting at my desk, motionless and sort of mesmerized by these small, trembling shadows. The shadows were *nothing*, actually, just short-lived flickerings of light and darkness, but for a few minutes this morning they were more important than anything I had come to my desk to do.

⋘ ⋙

## A WAVING LIFE

I noticed a branch waving in the wind outside this morning, and it seemed, somehow, to say something about my life. Indeed, there appears to be a lot of waving and shaking and swishing in these senior years of mine. People wave a hand my way, dogs wave their tails toward me, snowflakes in storms flutter as if waving their best wishes, and just now another branch seemed to beckon to me in the breeze. On the other hand, sometimes people wave aside my words, Social Security forms usually make sizable waves for me, and Delycia, as though she's catching a cab, sometimes has to wave me down to get my attention, which only makes my heart flutter like a waving flag even more for love of her.

✐ ✐

## SHEPHERDS ON THE PHONE

I've always enjoyed the fact that the good news of Christmas was first announced to simple, working-class shepherds, instead of tycoons or celebrities. It reminds me, at this time of year, that simplicity and ordinariness are more beautiful than splendor and grandiosity. My wife and I sometimes deal with a wonderful kind of simplicity and ordinariness when we talk on the phone with customer service representatives. It's not always the case, but usually the representatives show us the kind of patience and graciousness you might expect from best friends. They speak with gentleness and kindness, carefully finding answers to our often complicated questions. They're probably fairly low on the salary scale of their companies, but for us, these courteous phone workers sometimes make little miracles. I guess, in a way, they're like the simple shepherds of the Christmas story, just quietly doing their unnoticed but essential work, and we always try to give them our own kind of "good news" at the end of the conversation. We ask to speak to their superiors in order to say how grateful we are for their attentive service. We tell their superiors that these employees of theirs, in a straightforward, unassuming, skillful, and considerate manner, both answered our questions and warmed our hearts.

## A LITTLE APPLAUSE AND ACCLAIM

In the "Silver Sneakers" senior citizen exercise class Delycia and I are taking, we occasionally hear shouts of praise from our instructor, and it's surprising to me how heartening that can be. When I'm struggling to send my arms and legs where they're supposed to be going, when my feet can't seem to find a way to work appropriately, and when the thought crosses my mind to simply make an end to this nonsense, I sometimes hear a strong "Good work!" from the front of the room, or a sincere-sounding "Nice job, everyone!" Our teacher is working hard herself in front of us to do the exercises she asks us to do, but she seems to understand that part of her work is to praise her students. She knows, I guess, that nothing lifts a disheartened spirit like sincere acclaim. Indeed, it was amazing to me how a few forceful words of commendation could create a breeze of purposefulness and desire where there was only the weariness of discouragement. I started listening for her uplifting words. When I was winded and wheezing, I waited, and some shout of support from this stirring teacher always came.

## SHYNESS AND QUIET DAYS

Sometimes I think my granddaughter is simply shy, but sometimes I know that what we call shyness is never simple. Perhaps a person we call shy might just be like a silent, peaceful day, the kind we love for its serenity. Ava might be a person who's pleased to share her peacefulness in a hushed, unspoken way – not always throwing her arms around everyone, but simply sharing the sunshine of her life by being with us in her quiet manner. The dawn of a lovely day doesn't dash up to greet us, but gently presents itself in its settled way, and so does Ava. When Delycia and I arrive for a visit, there she is, standing unassuming and silent, with a modest but shining smile. She's shy, perhaps, but shy like sunlight on a mild morning.

## SILENT BREAKFASTS

At a retreat center we are visiting now, breakfasts in the main dining room are silent, something I haven't experienced since my seminary days 50-some years ago, and so far the silence has been not only bearable, but thoroughly enjoyable. It's given me the chance to choose what thoughts to think, to slowly select something to consider as I eat instead of scurrying madly among thoughts as they stampede through me. My mind is usually a crazy place in the morning, and the silence here has allowed me to sort my early thoughts out, to set them apart and see them clearly with my coffee, tofu, and toast. It has made the meal more like a trouble-free reflection than a quick gulping down and getting on with the day. It's also been inspiring to see so many people sitting silently with their food, eating with thoughtfulness and perhaps understanding. In a world widely shaken by the noise of misfortune, here are people taking pleasure in silence, eating and drinking with quiet delight. Here is a morning meal made of stillness and appreciation.

## SILVER AND GOLD

Delycia and I don't have an overflowing amount of money, and no silver and gold, but we do sometimes stop and consider – and *marvel* – at how really rich we are. Riding on this sleek, astonishing planet day after day is enough in itself to make a person feel afflu-ent. We're prosperous because this earth is prosperous. It overflows with wealth for us -- air to breathe, food to eat, and scenes more special than solid investments. Last evening, we saw something from our windows, something way better than silver and gold – a line of softly glowing clouds spread across the west as the sun was sinking. A recession can't take that kind of wealth away. Beauty like that shines way brighter than a bank account.

# LIVING LIKE LEAVES

As I was watching some leaves skipping in the wind this way and that across the grass this morning, I thought about the back-and-forth skipping my life often does. Time and again, I seem to bounce around from plan to plan, promise to promise, goal to goal – happily giving myself permission to change my mind, double back, rethink things, take a new trail. One fine idea gives way to a finer one. One second I decide to take the trash out, but then, in a flash, I decide to do the dishes instead. At 9:00 I know exactly what I want to do this afternoon, but at 9:01 a different and more wonderful plan appears. Back and forth, here and there, this and that, one thing and then another. Leaves let themselves loose to the winds, and so, sometimes, do I. Life shifts and skips second by second, and occasionally – usually with a smile – so do I.

---

## SLICKNESS

There's something strange about slickness – how skiers and sledders absolutely love it, but drivers on icy roads despise it. We drove on slick roads this morning, making our way north to our granddaughter's school in Brooklyn (CT) for some special 1st grade performances. Delycia is a skilled and cautious driver, but I still felt like our lives were unfastened and at risk as we drove along the snowy roads. Perhaps skiers feel a similar sense of hazard as they race down slippery mountains, but they probably love that feeling of carelessness and liberty. I must admit to feeling, on the icy interstate this morning, a certain amount of apprehension, but I also felt something like a sledder's high spirits. On a sled as a kid, danger didn't exist for me, and at 72, I sat back today and almost took pleasure in the adventure of moving carefully and successfully on frozen roads. I think, though, that we both were glad to finally get off the cold roads and into Ava's comfortable classroom where nothing was perilous and all was delight.

<hr>

## SLIVERS AND SPECKS

I saw a sliver of a moon above the house early this morning, just a shaving of silver light in a dark sunrise sky, and it started me thinking about other slivers, other shreds of things I've come across. So much of my life, in fact, seems made up of these kinds of small, flake-like things, mere scraps of experience, that often pass unnoticed. Someone passing me on the street, for instance, or a piece of a breeze wandering past the house, or a fragment of a few words heard in the supermarket – these are slivers like this morning's small moon above the house, just slight little experiences that sometimes disappear unseen and unappreciated. Even happiness, I guess, is like this – presented to me mostly in bits and snippets that can sail right past me if I'm not alert. I was lucky to look up this morning to see the silver flake of the moon, and hopefully I'll be lucky, too, to see the small pieces of happiness strewn around me today.

⊷⊶

## SLOW DRIVING, SLOW READING

On the road I sometimes find myself behind a slow driver, and within seconds I'm usually simmering a little, much the way my students probably simmered when I made them read very slowly -- actually *study* -- a book like *To Kill a Mockingbird*, paragraph by paragraph, sentence by sentence, sometimes even word by word. Many of the students, I feel sure, would have liked to rush through the plot of Lee's novel as quickly as possible and then rush on to the next book, just as, when I find myself slowed almost to a standstill behind a leisurely driver, I grow anxious to push on with the business of the day. Like most of us, I want to get where I'm going quickly so I can quickly get to my next goal, and my next, and on and on, and I think many of my students thought of reading in a similar way. They were accustomed, perhaps, to reading a novel mostly to find out what happens, and then, when it's finished, starting another one to find out what happens, and so on and so on. Things were very different in my rather measured and deliberate English class, and I sometimes saw, with surprise, the similarity between languid, dilly-dallying drivers and my own teaching methods. A sluggish driver ahead of me was like old Mr. Salsich and his infamously slow style of both reading and teaching. The slow-moving driver made me slow way down so I had nothing better to do than take pleasure in the drive, and I made my students slow down as they traveled through the pages of Harper Lee's beautiful novel. Sometimes, in fact, we came to a momentary halt among some splendid sentences; indeed, sometimes we even stopped to observe and discuss a single paragraph for an entire class period! "Let's get going!" my students must have been silently screaming as the minutes crept along with the English class bus remaining at a standstill beside a few sentences, and I want to yell something similar as I crawl along behind an unhurried and perfectly satisfied driver.

━┼╌ ┼╌━

## EVERYDAY MAJESTY

In the winter, majesty makes itself known in a number of simple ways. There's the whiteness of snow, for instance – a widespread and stately presence that's all around us some days. Delycia and I often visit friends in the snowy regions of northern New England, and the sunlight on the snow always makes it shine in a resplendent way. There's something solemn about the New Hampshire hills when they're wrapped in robes of snow, almost as if they're the home of kings and queens, with unseen sumptuous snow castles somewhere among them. I also notice, in all seasons, the majesty of simple people showing their graciousness – an older couple sitting as dignified as a duke and duchess, a man wearing his coat in a kingly way, a woman steering her wheelchair with a certain kind of magnificence. Even the table in the mall where I'm writing this has a clean and correct appearance, as if prepared for a prince, perhaps even a somewhat shabby but spirited senior-citizen prince waiting for his wife.

━┼╌ ┼╌━

## SLOW MOTION

I sometimes wonder if I could live, at least for a day, a sort of slow-motion life, like so many things I see around me. The flowers in Delycia's garden, for instance, grow so slowly in a day's time that no one notices it, and clouds cross the sky some days as slowly as dawn goes gradually across to darkness. Maybe I could make our bed in the morning somewhat the way flowers grow, setting out the sheets and straightening the bedspread with purposefulness. Perhaps I could wash the dishes the way clouds carry themselves, sort of floating through the job, unhurriedly going from glasses to cups to plates. Maybe I could even do my daily writing in a similar way, setting down the words little by little and lovingly, taking my time, making a paragraph as patiently as birds set sticks in their perfect places for a nest. It would be a way to live luxuriously, at least for a day, letting myself move like the nearby Mystic River, restfully and with perfect ease.

⚬

## SNOW, FLAMES, AND A PUZZLE

Outside, a billion big snowflakes are floating down on our neighborhood, while inside our snug house, the flames of an inviting fire are fluttering and leaping in the fireplace. There's a similar randomness in both – the snow sailing here and there, and the fire doing its dance in a thousand ways. There's also a jigsaw puzzle on the table not far from the fire, and lately the pieces have seemed as haphazard as the flames and the snowflakes. I know, though, that they'll all eventually fit together, just as the flames will eventually settle together into one smooth pile of ashes, and just as the snow, by sunrise, will be spread across the streets and yards in a single soft sheet.

⚬

## SO FAR, SO GOOD

Over the last several decades of my teaching career, the old pedagogical practice of praising students was severely disparaged in articles and books, but I must confess to always being fairly enthusiastic about it. I think my students, as individual persons, *deserved* to be praised – *all the time.* Certainly their actions sometimes deserved criticism, but their inner lives – their hearts and souls, you might say -- always deserved praise. In the most fundamental ways, they were good people. At every moment of every class, I could have said to each of the students, "so far, so good", because at that moment, as far as they had come on their life-long journey, they were *so* good, *so* just what they should have been at that instant. They may not have known how to use semicolons or what the symbolism of a James Joyce story means or how to listen carefully when the teacher is speaking, but for that specific moment of their lives, they were, in their own special ways, just right. I guess I've never believed in the linear theory of learning and human development. I didn't believe my students would necessarily be smarter students or better people tomorrow, or next year, or twenty years from now. Wisdom and graciousness don't grow gradually along a straight line. I knew teenage students who, in very real ways, were just as gifted and good and wise as 60-year-olds with advanced degrees. I suppose, when I think of the young people I taught, instead of a straight line I think of a circle of an infinite circumference, and each student is always at the center. No matter how many days or years pass, no matter what my former students do or how many books they read or how many courses they take, each of them will always, at each moment, be at the exact center of the universe – precisely where they should be. They will always have come *so* far, and be *so* good, and deserve *so* much praise.

⊶⊰⊱⊷

## SOARING IN CONNECTICUT

Yesterday I did some "soaring" of a surprising kind. When seagulls soar along the shore, they maintain height without flapping their wings – in other words, without working extra hard – and I soared in somewhat the same way at "Make We Joy", the winter solstice celebration at Connecticut College's Harkness Chapel. I was sitting beside Delycia, but I felt like I was flying for most of the hour, just floating along on the cheerful spirits arising from the singing and dancing. Like a seagull, I soared without exerting myself, gliding with no effort on an easygoing breeze of gladness. Then, in the evening, we saw Handel's Messiah performed at St. Patrick's Cathedral in Norwich, a building that soars in its own special way. Situated in a small, unexceptional city in New England, this church ascends in a spacious manner, the walls and pillars surging up to the impressive dome, and I did some surging myself as I listened to the performance. In my mind, in a lazy and loose way, I effortlessly rose and spiraled and coasted along on the music. The seagulls I've seen couldn't have done it any better.

❧ ❧

### SOFTLY FALLING THOUGHTS

Watching the snowflakes slowly falling this morning made me think of the countless thoughts that come drifting down on all of us in their soft but insistent way. We truly live in the midst of a steady snowfall of thoughts, all as soft as the snow descending among the trees outside our house. True, some of my thoughts – those filled with stress or uneasiness – don't seem especially soft, but perhaps that's because I feel like I'm being besieged by the thoughts, right in the center of them, instead of observing them from a safe distance. When unsettling thoughts seem to be filling my mind, perhaps I can learn to take a few (or maybe many) steps back and dispassionately survey them as they flutter inside me, simply taking notice of the thoughts instead of being "snowed under" by them. Then, maybe those distressing thoughts might seem as harmless as

157

the snowflakes floating past our windows just now. Snowflakes soon dissolve and disappear, and so, sooner or later, do all thoughts, stressful ones included.

⟩⟨ ⟩⟨

## A MOUNTAIN FULL OF HORSES

When I feel fearful, I often think of an old story about a guy who thought he was surrounded by enemies, but then a friend said the mountains around him were not full of enemies, but rather of friendly horses and riders ready to help. I need to see those horses clearly – to see that life is way more full of friendship and assistance than hostility and restraint. Support, not hindrance, always surrounds me. Like the guy in the story, I need to open my eyes in a new way and know the safety that always encircles me.

⟩⟨ ⟩⟨

# NOTHING REALLY MATTERS

S omeone once said that *everything should be honored, but nothing really matters* – a truth I have been thinking a lot about lately. Yesterday afternoon I was standing outside in breezy spring sunshine, and I thought, yes, everything *should* be honored – these sunlit minutes on the lawn, but also all the troublesome and sorrowful times, all the seeming misfortunes. Every event, every situation, every person, every thought, every single moment, should be respected as though it is a precious miracle, because it *is*. Whatever the universe unfolds for us (whether we label it "good" or "bad") is a marvel worth our respect. This doesn't mean, though, that anything really "matters", or at least that any one part of creation matters more than any other. In the kind of Universe that we live in, which is endlessly intricate but also one hundred percent harmonious, no facet of it is more important than any other. Everything, from the farthest star to the most miniscule atom, is of equal value and significance. Everything matters equally, which, in a sense, means nothing *really* matters, or matters more than anything else.

All that truly matters is the completely cohesive and harmonious universe, which has been successfully fashioning and re-fashioning itself for numberless eons, and which will continue to do so into infinity. Instead of thinking I have to fret and fuss about each present moment because everything matters, I should focus my attention on cherishing the astonishing creations of the universe. Instead of taking things seriously, I should take them reverently and gratefully.

―――

## SOONER OR LATER

Sometimes, when morning mist is spread over Mystic, I think of the many times when mist seemed to make its way across my teaching – times when all I could see as I was standing before my students was the haze of imprecise lesson plans and sleepy students. Those were the days when doing my job seemed similar to searching for a certain small stone in a vast forest. On those confused classroom days, try as I might, I saw no signals ahead to help me make the most of whatever lesson plan I had prepared. All was confusion and indecision. I guess what I needed to remember was that, like misty mornings hereabouts, things usually sort themselves out, and light eventually lets itself through. Almost always the mist where we live disappears by noon, and a rousing sunshine spreads around us. In its leisurely way, nature alters our world from gray to something closer to gold, and after a mist-filled morning, I'm sometimes walking a sunny beach by three. The lesson in all this? In my just-starting retirement, if a misty kind of confusion settles upon me, I should simply sit back and be patient and prepare for some eventual mental sunshine. It always comes, just like the sun shows itself, sooner or later, in this small seashore town.

―――

## SPRINGING OUT AND UP

When I was a small boy, my friends and I sometimes played hide-and-seek, and the fun part was to spring out and scare the seeker. I also loved springing up on our family's trampoline, bouncing as high as I could, maybe even touching the tree limb above. I was thinking of this kind of young-at-heart happiness this morning because it's the first day of spring, the season when all things seem to spring out and up. Yesterday Delycia discovered some daffodil shoots standing straight and strong amidst the last of the snow, as if they had just sprung up to sing their warmhearted song to winter. Also, in the next few weeks I'm sure some warm days will spring out on us by surprise, as if they've been hiding and hoping they could pleasantly shock us with soft winds and sunshine. Best of all, I think, are the pleasant feelings that seem to spring up inside us at this time of year, feelings that lift us up so we can touch the topmost possibilities of just plain pleasure and satisfaction.

## EVER-PRESENT IMPROVISATION

On this spring morning, I'm marveling at the improvisational skills I see around me outside. Everything seems to be happening spontaneously – the patio umbrella bowing in the wind in random ways, the hanging bird feeders floating this way and that, cars coming haphazardly past the house, thoughts arbitrarily blooming in my mind. It seems to be a random world in our backyard today, but it's a lovely, logical kind of randomness. No doubt there's a purpose behind all the spur-of-the-moment rippling and floating and waving and whisking I'm seeing, but it seems to be a kind of boundless and free-wheeling purpose, like dancers with blissful abandon doing just what occurs to them.

## GREAT STORIES

I was saying to Delycia several days ago that the recent events in the life of one of our friends would make a great story, and shortly after, I fell to thinking about some other great stories surrounding us. There's the story of why the sun shines the way it does day after day, the story of how night knows just when to start its stars shining, the story of this spinning, handsome earth and its inhabitants, the story of a single spider on a shaking web beside the house. There's the story of how a new breath brings new life to our lungs, the story of our muscles somehow showing our bodies how to move, and the story of our bones bearing our weight with reasonable ease. These are stunning little everyday stories that make my life, and Delycia's, and *all* lives, truly great in strange and distinguishing ways.

## STANDING STILL

I should be standing still more often these days. I should stop doing things now and then and simply stay where I am in absolute stillness, like a tree that just stands where it is, or like birds that seem to stay silently on wires and tree limbs for many minutes. Very few times in my life have I stood still just for the sake of the peace and serenity of it – just stopped doing things and simply looked and listened because it's good to look and listen. Perhaps, in future days, I should occasionally stand in our backyard, silent and still for a few minutes, making myself truly see and hear what's around me. Perhaps I should be like a statue in the sunshine, so hushed and stock-still the birds might bring themselves to rest in my shadow. I should be an old guy gone silent and stationary for once in his life, just breathing and looking and listening.

# STAYING

I would like to learn to "stay" more often, to remain right where
I am without wandering off to some other place or task. There's
something special, I think, about staying put. Stones do it constantly and easily, just sticking to where they are for months and
maybe years and centuries and eons. The stones in our stone wall
have stayed there for years, precisely where they were placed, and
stones in fields have been quietly sitting in the same places for perhaps hundreds of years. Maybe I'll try a little staying today – just
letting myself be left somewhere to sit silently, to persist in being
just where I am, to suspend all stirring and rushing and just stay, a
senior-citizen stone sitting in peace.

❧

## STEADFASTNESS

Each day I search for what I might call steadfastness, and it's usually easy to find. I see it in the trustworthy sun that always shows
up when it's supposed to. For billions of years, no matter what

muddles our human world might be in, the sun has reliably risen each morning to make a new start for us. I see it also, as I look out each morning, in the true and constant trees on our street. A few, I'm sure, have been faithfully there for more years than I've been alive, and all of them have been standing in a resolute way for the two years of our residence on this street. And speaking of resoluteness, where can it be found more unfailingly than in my own breath, coming in and out in its unwavering way moment after moment after moment? Even when my world seems to have been temporarily torn apart, my breath, my steady friend, still faithfully sends me fresh oxygen, fresh opportunities to be strong. All I need to do is stay quiet in the storm and listen to my breathing, the trusty team leader of my little life, as it keeps bringing its gifts.

━┥ ┝━

## BALLET ALL AROUND

After seeing a wonderful performance by The Boston Ballet one afternoon, I saw another dance presentation outside Boston's South Station. As Delycia and I sat outside on a bench in a soft but steady breeze waiting for our train, I saw a piece of paper tumbling across the sidewalk with what seemed like simple gracefulness, and some limbs above us were smoothly swaying and bending. Delycia had some shopping bags, and they shook in the breeze in seemingly stylish ways, and soon I noticed a woman walking in a lively style, working with the breeze with straightforward smoothness and ease, moving her arms with a sort of everyday finesse. And just before we boarded the train, a guy walked past us in a slow saunter, arms swinging and head tossing in the breeze in fine fashion. He was definitely a dancer – less practiced and seasoned, perhaps, than the ballet dancers earlier in the afternoon, but somehow just as pleasing.

━┥ ┝━

## BEING AVAILABLE
### (written on Thanksgiving Day)

On this special day, as I give thanks, I want to also promise, again, to be available to people. The word "avail" derives from the Latin word meaning "be of value, be strong", and that's how I want to be for the people in my life. I want to be of some use to them, if it only means stopping in for a visit, or sending a sunny note, or just being still and listening. I want to stay near and stay strong for them. I want them to know I am always free and unoccupied when they need me, always at hand, always handy and at their disposal, always available.

━━┿ ┿━━

## RISING
### (written on Christmas Day)

Many things are rising this morning – sunshine among the silent trees, flocks of geese going south, flames in a stone fireplace, and warm feelings in our family. Delycia and I are at Jamie's with Amy, Matt, Noah, and Ava for our Christmas celebration, and good spirits are all around the house, and rising. Right now, I'm sitting beside the soaring Christmas tree (11 feet, at least), and this life I'm lucky to be living seems to have shot up higher than ever. I've ridden the elevator of good fortune to the top floor. Just now a flame in the fireplace leaped higher than it seemed possible, and I've named it Hamilton.

━━┿ ┿━━

## STEADILY, GENTLY, QUIETLY

During a break in today's classes, I leaned back in my chair and watched a few leaves drop, now and then, from a tree beside my classroom. It was a nearly windless day, so the old, well-wrinkled leaves fell at a leisurely pace, one by one. It sometimes seemed like several minutes would pass before another leaf would softly sail down to the ground. It got me thinking about teaching. I realized that leaves fall only when they are totally ready to fall, when their exact time has come. There's no rushing involved, but rather a great sense of patience and certainty. The leaves will fall when they will. Unlike our human world of relentless haste and stress, the tree and its leaves live lives of calm, inescapable sureness – a quality I would like to see more of in my teaching. As I watched the tree, and waited for my next class to assemble, I hoped I might teach them just the way the leaves were falling -- steadily, gently, and quietly.

⊷⊶

## STIFF ARMS OR WHIRLS

For most of my life, I have been using the old "stiff arm" strategy from my football days to push away what I saw as problems, but these days some occasional twists and pivots seem to be working just as well. Instead of shoving aside my so-called problems, I'm seeing that I can usually swirl around them with something like a smile. Instead of shoves and thrusts, I've been using more spins and whirls, more loose and limber versatility as a way of passing through my problems. It seems, in these first years of my 70's, that life is a lot more like a dance than a dispute. There's more billowing in it than forcing and thrusting. It's not that I ignore the usual difficulties of life, just that I roll *with* them rather than ram against them. I *flow* a lot more than I force. I almost hear the cheers in the stands as I swivel past all these amateurish, incompetent problems.

⊷⊶

## TWO OLD DOGS

I once knew an old German shepherd made of both bravery and kindness. He was bold, but when someone needed friendship, he was as soft as April days. He threw himself at all threats, but sat down in silence beside lonesome folks. I was thinking of this old dog recently when I needed both the courage to argue against a gloomy friend's pessimism and the kindness to console him. It's not easy to be a fighter against gloominess and also a comforting friend, but if that old dog could do it, so, perhaps, can this one.

⇒⊢ ⊣⇐

## SUDDEN YOUTHFULNESS

"As for the [old woman], she took on a sudden look of youth; you felt as if she promised a great future, and was beginning, not ending ..."

-- Sarah Orne Jewett, *The Country of the Pointed Firs*

Every so often I have a feeling of sudden youthfulness, as if I'm 6 instead of 73, as if spring is just starting in me as well as in the trees beside our house. This feeling flows from some place that's a mystery to me, somewhere as near as my heart and as far off as the farthest stars, and I'm never sure when it will show up. Sometimes the feeling starts when I'm eating something special and sensing how young the universe is and how really young my life is. Or it might begin when I'm breathing hard on my bike on far-reaching roads on days that sing of cleanness and new starts. Sometimes it's only a little feeling, but one that finds me just when I most need to feel fresh and unfenced, when I most need to notice the childish

shine on my hands. Since, like all of us, I have this kind of innocence deep inside me, all I need to do is see it and accept it, and
then let my life leap around like the young thing it always truly is.

# SUNRISES

S ometimes I think of the several kinds of sunrises I could see
every day – every hour, I guess. You might say there's a rising
sun inside all the moments that make their fresh starts so many
times a day. All the moments that come to pass carry cleanness
and brilliance as special as any sunrise, if only I could notice it.
It's as if there's a new-made morning in every passing moment – a
chance to choose light instead of darkness, confidence instead of
cynicism, the glow of hopefulness instead of the shadows of dis-
trust. Tens of thousands of times each day, I could create a sunrise
for myself by simply seeing the newness that's rising around me. It
would be easy, like looking for gold in a land of gold, or searching
for warmth on a sunny shore.

⊨+ +⊫

## SUNSHINE AND WIND AND I
When I look in the mirror, I don't see sunshine and wind, and yet,
in a sense, that's what's there. The atoms that swirl in sunshine

169

and wind are the same ones that shape my bones and blood. The atoms in my bloodstream were made as many billions of years ago as those in the sun I see rising outside my house this morning, and the timeless winds are no older than the calcium I carry inside me. Sunshine and wind and I are inseparable pieces of the single, immeasurable universe. We three mix and mingle as surely as the breezes across our yards, as surely as the seamless rays of sunshine. The separate person I seem to see in the mirror is no more separate than one swirl of the wind is separate from another, or one shaft of sunlight is separate from another. We shine and swirl together, sunshine and wind and I.

---

## YIELDING

Oddly enough, I actually look forward to seeing YIELD signs on the road when I'm driving, for they afford me a chance to once again surrender, something I mostly missed out on in my younger years. I grew up in a culture that equated surrendering with defeat and disgrace, so I became, like most of the guys I grew up with, a "fighter", someone who tried to never give in or give up. As the years passed, however, I slowly saw that surrendering sometimes brings conquest instead of defeat, sometimes shows strength instead of weakness. Rivers, after all, surrender to boulders and thus easily flow around them, and winds give in to mountains and thereby blow right by them. I see now that submitting can sometimes strengthen a person, and giving way can often get you a victory. I guess I've learned, over the years, that treating life like a war is a woeful way to live. I've set down my weapons, you might say. I'm yielding more often to the flow of life – and of cars. I'm raising the white flag, and finding much more force and joyfulness because of it.

---

## A SWEET-TEMPERED BOXER

"So complete is his acquiescence . . . [his] pugnacious acceptance of reality ..."

-- Michael Sadlier, in *Anthony Trollope: A Commentary*

Until I read Mr. Sadlier's essay, I would never have considered using the words "acquiescence" and "pugnacious" together in a discussion of how to live a good life, but he used them so appropriately in his treatise on the Victorian novelist that I begin wondering whether a truly successful person has to be, you might say, *pugnaciously acquiescent*. It's thought-provoking that the word "acquiesce" derives from the Latin word for "quiet", for it suggests that an acquiescent person is simply one who finds more reasons for inner peace than for unease and apprehension. The word literally means "to be at rest", which summons up a picture of a person who treats whatever happens in life as a noteworthy occurrence that should be quietly welcomed and walked around and appraised. This is a person who knows that little can be gained by giving battle, but that surprising strength can be gained through simple acceptance. I'm not speaking about a submissive and spineless acceptance, but rather a *pugnacious* one – the kind of acquiescence that says, in soft but spirited tones, "Yes, I'm brave enough to say yes to life as it shows itself to me, life as it is." It's a courageous kind of acquiescence, a willingness to wonder and marvel at life's occurrences rather than condemn and castigate them. Of course, there will be times when, for one reason or another, events will deserve a person's censure, but the censure should be given with the same humble acquiescence -- the same sense of quietly accepting what simply needs to be done. A person can be both tough and soft, both stern and merciful. It's like being sweet-tempered, but with boxing gloves on.

## SWIFT TO HEAR

I recall my father encouraging me to - as he put it - "be swift to hear and slow to speak", and sometimes, at 73, I still see little progress in myself in these areas. I'm still fairly slow to settle down and truly listen to someone – slow to show people that I sincerely care about what they are saying. I *act* like I'm listening, true, but often my mind makes excursions in all kinds of directions rather than actually staying with what is being said to me. My dad would be disappointed to know that I'm definitely swift to speak, but not so often willing to wait patiently, stay silent, and actually listen to what someone is saying. I love his idea of being "swift to hear". I want to be able to suddenly stop everything in order to truly listen. I want to be brisk in bringing my attention when a person is speaking to me. These days, I like to live in a laid-back way, but when I'm listening to someone, I want to be swift with my kindness and care.

***

## SECRET RHYTHMS

Not long ago, Delycia and I participated in a drumming circle at a yoga center, and the rhythms we worked with called to mind some rhythms I almost never notice in my on-the-go life. There's the rhythm, for instance, of my rising and falling heart as it manages the music of my body. My life moves in a steady, reassuring cadence that I rarely recognize, and most of it is made by my heart. Something similar to songs sing inside me every second, the songs of a musical heart and the blood borne along by its steady beat. I would do well to wait, every so often, and listen to this quiet tempo inside me. I could also listen more alertly to the rhythms of the thoughts that pass through me. They're always flowing – cheerful thoughts and sad ones, uplifting thoughts and lonely ones – and they do seem to move at a reasonably steady rhythm. It's as if my thoughts are part of a song continuously sung to me by the universe, a song I rarely notice, a song as pulsating and surprising as the sounds of the drumming circle.

⊨⊣⊦⊨

## MORNING ASTONISHMENT

Sometimes, usually in the early morning, a feeling of absolute astonishment comes over me, a sense that my situation in life is indescribably miraculous. I find myself asking, as I did this morning, how I happen to be lucky enough to be located at this moment in time on a smoothly spinning planet in an astonishingly large galaxy in a universe of unthinkable numbers of such galaxies. I find myself marveling at the smallest things – the way the wind, as I write, is furling and unfurling our flag in countless ways; the way our neighbor's red car is shining in the sunlight; the way Delycia is smoothly turning the pages of a calendar in the kitchen. I'm sometimes almost stock-still with wonder. How, I ask, does my life-giving breath keep coming and going? How do I have many thousands of new thoughts each day, totaling many millions in my lifetime? And where do all these thoughts come from? And where do gentleness and generosity and kindness come from, and how did they become infinite and imperishable?

⊨⊣⊦⊨

## MUCH LOVE

Good friends sometimes close a letter with "much love", and just now, on another frozen, snowbound day in Mystic, I see much love all around me. I see it in my wife's purple orchids carrying themselves with great grace on a window shelf near where I'm typing.

173

They were set there months ago because Delycia does more loving than anyone I know, and now the blossoms are beautifying both our home and the snowy scene outside the window. I see love, too, in the pendulum clock hanging on the wall behind me – a clock made by craftsmen who probably loved their labor, loved setting the parts in their proper places so the chimes would reliably sing their song every fifteen minutes. When you love your work, the love lives on in your creations, and this is true even for the cold, old streets of our town which have been dependably plowed, over and over this winter, by drivers who do their work with precision, and perhaps (I hope) with pride. They may not see it this way, but I see much love in what they have done for all of us, allowing us to move about town and take this fairly wild winter in stride, and maybe even in occasional joyfulness.

⚓

## A REALLY OLD YOUNG GUY

I am legally 73 years old, but according to an astrophysicist friend of mine, I've been around for billions of years. In fact, I'm not just a senior citizen, but a truly ancient guy, as old as the stars. Scientific studies say that my body is composed of approximately 7,000,000,000,000,000,000,000,000,000 atoms, most of which, my friend tells me, came into being when giant stars exploded several billion years ago. Apparently these atoms browsed around the universe for eons before they somehow assembled and settled together in 1941 to produce an arrangement that became known as "Hamilton Salsich". Who knows -- some of my atoms might have made up parts of prehistoric mountains or the kidney of a king or a wee shrew's eyes before they luckily linked up to bring a baby to life in St. Louis 73 years ago. What's equally amazing is that some studies suggest that the 37 trillion cells in my body are replaced with brand new ones about every ten years, which means, unless I'm missing something, that my body is now only about 10 years old. If I understand this correctly, I've been around for billions of years, but am still just a 10-year-old kid. I'm ancient, but still – literally – in the springtime of life.

# THE FIRE HAD NO POWER

I try to avoid using the word "God", since its meaning has become so fuzzy over the centuries, but there surely is a non-material force (or Force) in the universe that, again and again down through history, has allowed gentleness and serenity to overcome fear and affliction. Occasionally I think about the Bible story of the men who survived being thrown into a fiery furnace, and I start to wonder: What future fires, what pain and grief, may await me, and will I be able to survive, and even, as the boys in the story did, somehow *flourish* inside the flames of my suffering? Will I be able to face future troubles with poise and inner stillness, not by pretending the troubles don't exist, but by understanding that there's a calming and loving force in the universe that's far stronger than any suffering I might experience? I think of the Bible story as an allegory, in which the fiery furnace stands for any situation that seems to surround us with hopelessness. Somehow the men in the story were able to feel fully the power of unison and peace that pervades the universe, from the farthest star to the smallest cell in our bodies, and somehow that power easily erased the disharmony of their situation. The fire in their lives had no power when put up against the non-material power of peacefulness, and I hope that will be true of the various physical and emotional fires that will surely flare up in my life in years to come.

═╪╪═

## AN EVER-PRESENT POWER
It sometimes surprises me that I don't ever seem to find myself far from the presence of goodness. It's always close by, like an ever-present power, like a gracious and supportive spirit. No matter how bad things seem to get, goodness is always nearby -- perhaps in the smile of someone at the grocery store, perhaps in a wave from a walker passing the house, perhaps simply in the quiet look of clouds coming across the trees. It seems omnipresent, this universal force that stays beside us through the worst adversities. When sorrow closes in, goodness gets its light ready. When hatred stirs up its short-lived bedlam, goodness, somewhere close by, prepares its gentle but far superior powers.

═╪╪═

## THE FURIOUS SERENITY OF SPARROWS
It's fun to see so many sparrows swirling around our feeders these days, and doing it with a kind of furious serenity. They seem zestful in an unruffled way as they flutter and quiver and peck out some seeds and soar off again. There's a sort of peaceful fury in their motions, a tumultuous calmness that amazes me as I watch. They move their heads in jerky ways, but even this nervous way of turning seems to be done in an unflustered manner, sort of the way leaves can shake in a storm with utter gracefulness. What I love most is the way a group of them can suddenly soar off to nearby bushes in what seems like a perfect flight pattern. They fly off quickly but

beautifully, flashing away in what always looks like elegant orderliness. I'd love to see, in my sometimes busy days, the shipshape neatness I see in these birds' frantic dancing around the feeders. It wouldn't be bad to live with the disciplined liveliness of sparrows.

---

## THE GOOD NEW DAYS

I've often heard people speak of "the good old days", as though something wonderful was almost always happening back then, but this morning, when I noticed the sunlight spread so smoothly across the snow, I started thinking about this good *new* day, and all the good new days that lie ahead. There's so much that I miss in each new moment, and sometimes it's because I'm lost somewhere back in the old days, dreaming of the supposed simplicity of life back when things were – or at least seemed – less bewildering and more straightforward. What's strange about this is that there is nothing less bewildering or more straightforward than the winter sunshine that gave a sheen to the snow-cover this morning and made it glisten. Nor could there have been anything lovelier in the old days than the flames in our fireplace just now, shaking and swaying and sending warmth our way on this frosty day. Like all days, this is *a good new day*. I'm trying lately to let the good old days lie where they are, far off in my memories, and prepare myself to better appreciate the good new miracles made right before my eyes, new day by new day.

---

## THE INVISIBLE WORLD IN ENGLISH CLASS

In Book 6 of *The Prelude,* the poet William Wordsworth writes of "a flash that ... revealed / The invisible world", and it occurs to me that it might be the kind of flash that happened occasionally in my English classes. It's a fact that English teachers and their students, since they work mainly with words and ideas, often concern them-selves with the hidden, the masked, the invisible. There are times when they're like explorers in the world of the unseen. In a way, they are part-time clairvoyants, using a human being's peculiar ability to see beyond normal sensory contact – in their case, beyond the outer shell of words on a page and into the concealed country of their meanings. Of course, English teachers and their students are visible as they sit at their desks in the classroom, and their tools are certainly visible – books, paper, pencils, digital devices -- but they do most of their labor in the kingdom of ideas, those ghostly gift-givers that flit through our lives with spirit and influence. A visitor to my classroom might have seen a fairly uninspiring sight – a group of teens and a bald guy quietly communicating with each other – but what they wouldn't have seen is what's special. Under the surface of the seemingly commonplace conversations, unseen ideas were danc-ing around, not because I was any better than any other English teacher, but because that's what happens when adults and kids con-verse about words written in wonderful books. It's like science fic-tion, really – a strange, clandestine universe just inside the doors of great books, and behind the doors of almost any English class.

⇥⇤

## THE LINGERING TOUCH

"To see the joy with which these elder kinsfolk and acquain-tances had looked in one another's faces, and the lingering touch of their friendly hands . . ."

--Sarah Orne Jewett, in *The Country of the Pointed Firs*

At our heartwarming family reunion this weekend, we "elder kins-folk and acquaintances" of the family cheered for each other in charming, cordial ways. The young people played and shouted among themselves, throwing aside any small concerns and easily embracing the happiness of the occasion, but I have a feeling that it was we older friends, Ann and Pete Salsich's daughters and sons and their spouses, who profited in the fullest measure from the inspiring occasion. Just the touch of so many brother and sister hands was uplifting, letting us know, over and over for three satisfying days, that we are first-class friends, in good times or troubles. As I type this at my seat on our homeward flight, I feel the "lingering touch" of those handshakes and hugs, freely offered symbols of fondness and fidelity that seemed stronger and more solicitous than ever. I see the sky outside the plane's window, and somehow it doesn't seem nearly as immeasurable as the friendship of my dearly loved dad and mom's family.

⇌ ⇋

## THE POWER OF GENTLENESS

There are many kinds of power, but to me, the power of gentleness is the greatest. Consider, for example, the forceful gentleness of a river. Water is one of the softest of all material things, and yet it can move trees and whole houses when it floods in the spring. This gentle substance that washes your dishes can effortlessly wash away an entire town in flood season. In addition, there is the gentle, persistent power of even the softest breeze. A cool breeze in the summer can refresh the lives (and nerves) of an entire town in a matter of minutes. One minute you're sweating and frustrated, and the next minute you're relishing your life while an easygoing breeze ruffles you're hair. And finally, the most valiant and most admirable people I know are also the gentlest. These are people who know that the most important battles are won by single-minded gentleness. Like rivers, these people flow softly along with colossal power. Like the breezes of summer, they change our lives with their stalwart and relentless gentleness.

⊯ ⊯

### THE SAME SONG

As I was hanging out clothes on the laundry line yesterday, somewhere a bird was singing the same simple song again and again, and for some reason, it started me thinking about how strong and everpresent simplicity is. Most of us, myself included, make life far more full of twists and turns than it actually is, and thus we miss the natural straightforwardness of things. This bird, with its simple song, seemed to be living its life with effortlessness, simply reciting the same nofrills melody over and over. It's as if it knew instinctively that satisfaction is something simple rather than convoluted, plain rather than fancy. It reminded me of a lesson I learned long ago, sort of another simple song – that kindness is always stronger than unhappiness. This is an uncomplicated fact, the opposite of the cluttered and confusing rules we sometimes try to follow. The plain fact is, that no matter how full of despair a situation seems to be, if I simply stay kind to others, and to myself, and yes, to the situation itself, the uncomplicated allure of life will soon make itself felt once more. Like the bird singing its same song yesterday, I should say this over and over – "kindness conquers unhappiness, kindness conquers unhappiness". The bird knows satisfaction can come in simple ways, and so should I.

⊯ ⊯

### THE SIGNIFICANT SKY

"Looking into Napoleon's eyes, Prince Andrei thought about the insignificance of grandeur, about the insignificance of life, the meaning of which no one could understand, and about the still greater insignificance of death, the meaning of which no one among the living could understand or explain."

-- Leo Tolstoy, *War and Peace*

Prince Andrei Bolkonsky has long hoped to experience the honors and triumphs of warfare, but here, after the Russian army's blood-spattered defeat at Austerlitz, he's seriously wounded and starting to see life in simpler, more startling ways. All the things he thought were important – pride, privilege, and fame among them – are now revealed as utterly trivial. All his plans for celebrated successes are now petty and pointless. What he notices, as he's lying on his back and bleeding on the battlefield, is simply the sky, and to him it is far more significant than any of his plans and hopes. His self-centered past seems over, and only the "lofty, infinite sky with clouds racing across it" seems special.

⟞⟝ ⟞⟝

## THE SKY OVER BLACK FRIDAY

It's strange to me that, on this day after Thanksgiving, in the midst of a swarm of scurrying cars, I happened to notice how serene the sky seemed. We were driving to visit friends near Boston, and, while the interstate was filled with a frantic kind of traffic, the blue sky seemed calm in its immensity. We and thousands of others were zooming, but the sky seemed to be resting. It seemed to be saying, "Let those people dash and scamper; I'll stay where I always stay." There was peace in the Black Friday sky. There was lightheartedness in the lines of slim clouds along the horizon, and the sky's endless blueness brought a peaceful feeling as Delycia steered us among the racing, shopper-filled cars.

⇥⊹⊢⇤

## THE SORROW OF THE WORLD

When I heard today that some good friends have suffered a great sorrow, it came to me that their sorrow belongs not just to them, but to all of us. Their sorrow is, you might say, the sorrow of the world. Sorrow, after all, is not a physical entity that can be possessed by a single person, the way you might possess clothes or a car. Sorrow is more like a mist that moves through millions of us at the same time, swirling and settling in different ways in each person. Some of us feel the sorrow of disappointment, some the sorrow of loss, others the sorrow of hopelessness, but, in a real sense, it's the same sorrow, the same numbing mist that's been evermore making its heartbreaking way across the earth. My friends are feeling the same sorrow that's being felt, as I write, the world over – the sorrow of Syria, the sorrow of widows and orphans and refugees, the sorrow of the lost and lonely, the abandoned and unnoticed. We all share this sorrow. It's not mine or yours or ours or theirs. My sorrowful friends live far away from me, but we're together in this sorrow – they and I and all our suffering sisters and brother across the earth.

⇥⊹⊢⇤

## THE STARTLED EARTH

It's easy for me to imagine the earth being startled sometimes, the way we are startled when something surprising happens. I wonder, for instance, if the earth is startled when a war breaks out across its surface, since, for most of its history, it has seen peace and unison holding sway. Yes, we humans have waged dreadful wars over the centuries, but their significance falls far short when compared to the countless but seldom publicized deeds done in the name of friendship and kindness. The violent wars have received the head-lines, but the peaceful work for the well-being of all people, the calm and loving campaigns to make daily life a more satisfying experience for everyone, have been *far* more influential. For every act of violence, there have been numberless acts of compassion and mercy, and for every death on a battlefield, there have been billions of small but life-giving acts of goodness. The earth has seen our brutality, but it has seen far more of our compassion and kindness. That's why, in the midst of eons of constructive harmony among humans, it might be somewhat startled when a war breaks out.

# STRONG SOFTNESS

For many years I thought strength was somehow akin to hardness, solidity, and stiffness, but now I see there's a very soft kind of strength in the universe. Just now, as I was writing, a jumbo jet floated across the distant sky, somehow held up by the soft air surrounding it. In some mysterious way, the air is able to carry this 100-ton load with seeming ease. This is softness showing its muscles. Perhaps even more inspiring is the strong softness found in certain people. I once knew a man whose body had wasted away until he was just a skeletal spirit as he lay on his hospital bed, and yet he had a heart soft enough to welcome any problem or person, and strong enough to thoroughly vanquish self-pity and pessimism. His body was softly drifting away to nothingness, but his spirit was more than sturdy enough to strengthen and inspire his many visitors. Like the satiny sky that easily lifts up the super-big bodies of planes, this dying man made carrying suffering seem as easy as smiling, which he seemed to be almost always doing.

## THE TRUSTWORTHY PRESENT

All of us hope for a few faithful friends in our lives, and, strange as it may sound, I've found one in the always-steadfast present moment. I've discovered, as the years have passed, that no matter how unstable and inconsistent my life might seem, there is one thing that is constantly beside me – the present moment. It's like a trusted friend, always there in all its fullness and vitality. The present moment is unfailing in its loyalty. Look where I might, I'll never find anything more reliable. It stays alongside me at all times in all circumstances, as if to say, "No matter what, I'm here for you." And it's essential that I remember that the present is, indeed, here *for me*. Since each moment can't be anything other than what it is, in that sense each moment is absolutely perfect, and thus it offers me, over and over, a flawless gift. Each moment can make my life better in some beautiful way, but I must make myself see its excellence, its totally reliable ability to unfold new miracles for my life. The present – or perhaps *The Present* would be the more proper way to put it – is as trusty and constant as a friend can be, and more commanding, more matchless, more perfect.

⊷⊶

## MY WHOLE FAMILY

Sometimes I feel far away from my extended family out in St. Louis, but at those times I try to remember that my whole family – my endless family, actually – is always with me. The Salsich family is just a small part of my whole family. I belong to the universe, not just the Salsichs. Among my many brothers and sisters are the stars and seas and rivers and white chairs on porches and pine trees and tables in living rooms – all the things made from the brother and sister atoms formed by the Big Bang some 15 billion years ago. Al and Pete and Joe and Mike are my brothers, but so are all the living things that share this earth's atmosphere. Barbara and Susie and Maysie and Cat are my sisters, but so are the birds that breathe in and breathe out in our backyard, and so are the gray grass blades just showing through the snow today. Yes, most of my human family seems far off in the Midwest, but fortunately for me, they and my whole, undivided, and never-ending family is actually forever with me.

＝✦ ✦＝

## THE DISREGARDED

Lately, I've been noticing, and thinking about, people who don't seem to be winners. I pass them each day, the people with forlorn looks and stooping shoulders, those for whom life seems to be an overwhelming weight. I see them in the news – the increasing numbers of those with no job, the vast numbers of impoverished families, the millions of forsaken refugees. They seem to be ever-present, these people who carry such distressing burdens on their shoulders, who seem to have totally lost the game of life. Sadly, when I was teaching, I saw them in my own classes, too, though certainly not to such extremes. I saw the kids who had no friends, who spent recess by themselves, lost in their own breakable worlds. I saw the students who never seemed to "make it" in school, the ones who got C's semester after semester, who never seemed to be "winners" at anything. Sadly, it's so easy to fail to notice these kids. The winners -- the 'A' students, the class leaders, the well-liked kids -- take up so much of the spotlight that the ordinary, everyday students often get left outside of the light. Like the outcasts of the world – the homeless, the poor, the peculiar – these disregarded students must always struggle by themselves to bring some small, unnoticed distinction to their lives.

＝✦ ✦＝

## THERE IS A RIVER

When my students, like most of us, occasionally fall into dismay and discouragement, I always hope they will soon be able to see the river of good thoughts that's constantly flowing inside them. There is, indeed, a river there, and in all of us, and it has more rousing and optimistic ideas than we could ever count. It flows from somewhere or nowhere in its relentless manner, and the only way we don't notice it is by turning away and noticing the pessimistic river instead – a steady and persuasive one, for sure. It's easy for kids, in their sometimes frenzied and snarled lives, to be spellbound by the flow of downright depressing news and thoughts that pour past them, which is probably why I tried to select books to read in my English class that would bring a brighter view. I don't mean that I avoided books that showed the certainty of sorrow in human life, just that I looked for books that also showed the strength and inspiration that can come with, and even be created by, the sorrow. There is a river I love in great books, a river that carries light for the darkness and quiet confidence for the future, and those are the books that can be the creators of new life for young students, bringing a stream of stirring ideas that any teenager can make use of. Those are the books, too, that can turn the students back to the good river of hopeful thoughts that's always with us all, if we could only turn and see it.

⊷⊰⊱⊶

## THEY DON'T KNOW WHAT THEY'RE DOING

I am not a regular churchgoer, nor do I consider myself strictly a Christian, but during the days leading up to the celebration of Easter, I am always struck by what Jesus said in forgiving his enemies. He said he forgave them because "they don't know what they are doing", and when I read those words, I usually say to myself, "Yup, and neither do I." I do hundreds of things each day, from walking around the house and yard to setting words into sentences on this computer screen, and, honestly, I usually haven't a clue as to exactly what I'm doing. Life, to me, becomes more of a mystery with each passing day, and I often feel quite befuddled by what's happening. When I walk, for instance, what exactly are my muscles and bones and brain doing that enables me to move so efficiently? We use the word "walking" to conveniently label the activity, but that doesn't begin to describe the inconceivable complexity of it. And when I write, do I honestly have any clear idea what I'm doing? I like to *pretend* that I do, but in truth, the words seem to settle themselves across the screen in their own strange ways, with little help from me. The sentences sometimes seem clear, but I'm not at all sure how it happens. Actually, I guess something similar could be said about most of my life. I often feel like I'm living in the midst of a vast and generous (though not always happy) mystery, something like an endless rising of rainbows, or a continuous string of surprising sunsets. I could pause in amazement almost every moment of every day. Do I know what I'm doing, any more than the enemies of Jesus did? Usually not a bit. I just try to keep up with the spectacular show, and hope I'm no one's enemy.

⟱⟰

### LARGE HONORS

When a celebrity recently gave thanks for the "large honor" she had received, I started saying silent thanks for all kinds of large honors I've received. Starting with my surprising presence on a startling planet in a snug house with a beyond-belief wife who, lucky for me, loves me -- what larger honors could I receive? And each morning I wake up to a world of skies and trees and streets and houses and people and parades of endlessly strange present moments. Is this not a large daily honor for me? Also, I spent 45 years teaching teenagers, and I felt, almost from the start, that it was a high honor to walk into the classroom each morning. Each day, I felt like someone pinned an honorary medal on me and said, "You have been selected to receive the title of 'Teacher of Teenagers'. Be grateful for this great honor." I *was* grateful, always, and still am – grateful now, too, for the honor of being a bald, somewhat creased, but daring and cheerful senior citizen. It is indeed an honor to be 72. I say to all those 71-year-olds: Stay brave. One day you too might be honored with the shining "72 Years of Lucky Living" medal.

━━◈ ◈━━

## THOUGHTS ON VETERANS DAY

I am not a veteran, and, like most of us, I despise war, but this day, when we honor the men and women who served to keep safe our freedoms, is a very special one for me. I am beyond grateful for the liberty I am lucky to enjoy here, and for the faithful protection provided by our armed forces. I wish we didn't need women and men with weapons watching around the world to safeguard us from attack, but contempt and loathing for our country does exist, and I'm glad we have good soldiers, sailors, and flyers ready to fight for all of us. I'm lucky to live in a land where freedom can be found by anyone, and I give thanks today for that freedom's defenders.

━━◈ ◈━━

# TODAY NEEDS ME

Most of us probably have days when we feel sort of superfluous, like perhaps we're just an unnecessary speck in an immeasurable universe, but lucky for me, I usually wake up from that delusion fairly quickly, and recall, with a smile, that *today needs me.* Once again I see these simple but stunning truths – that this universe is endlessly harmonious and peaceable, that I am in no way separate from anything else in the universe, and that whatever I do today will significantly influence the entire universe. *I am needed today.* The oxygen atoms I send out from my lungs each second will he used again and again in countless ways by the universe. Every step I take will shift molecules around in ways that will slightly shift the stars and planets. My smiles could bring some sunshine to dark lives today. A word of thanks could throw a small blessing of light across someone's life on this exceptional day when, as usual, I and all of us are very much needed and necessary.

## TWO KINDS OF WAITING

It occurred to me this morning that there are two kinds of waiting, and I'm afraid I've spent far more time doing one kind than the other. The kind of waiting that turned into a routine for me in my younger days is like the waiting done by the man at the sheep market pool in the Bible's gospel of John. This man waited, just as I sometimes did, for a power outside himself to repair and revitalize something in his life. He apparently had felt powerless, and very ill, for 38 years, and each day he waited beside the presumably miraculous pool for some special material occurrence that he hoped would heal him. He was essentially imprisoned by his belief that the water of the pool had immense power and supervised his destiny. It was fortunate for him that Jesus passed by, because Jesus showed him, in a few simple words, a straightforward but stunning truth – a truth that transformed this waiting man's world. Jesus simply told the man that he was "whole". He made it clear to him that he was already, right at that moment, an essential part of an endless, unbroken, and harmonious marvel called life. What the man learned, and what I am still learning, is that we don't have to wait for salvation or healing or harmony or comfort or concord. All of these, in some form or another, are already present with me each moment, simply needing to be seen and embraced. The only kind of waiting I need to do today is the good and happy and breathless kind of waiting we all love. What hidden marvels of harmony and healing will unfold in the next moment, and the next, and the next? That's the question I need to ask myself all day today, and then wait with confidence for the answer to be revealed.

## A MINUET OF THOUGHTS

"... a state of mind liable to melt into a minuet with other states of mind, and to find itself bowing, smiling, and giving place with polite facility."

-- George Eliot, in *Middlemarch*

These words of George Eliot exactly describe the dance my own ideas seem to do. My mind is like an old English ballroom where ideas warmly move among each other in a peculiar kind of sociability and easiness. Thoughts of delight glide beside thoughts of fear, and beliefs that bad times are looming hold hands with beliefs that goodness is always nearby. What's especially interesting about this is that my thoughts can be so cordial to each other, like English lords and ladies letting their friendliness guide the flow of the dance. Perhaps if I would simply stand back and watch them, the thoughts that move through my mind might seem as graceful as the movements of eminent manor-house guests. If I stopped trying to always rule and regulate them, and gave up getting in fights with them, I might be able to enjoy the pleasant movements of my thoughts, their stylish steps and swings.

⚔️ ⚔️

## UNCONQUERABLE GENTLENESS

Sometimes the power of storms or cruelty or economic crashes can seem overwhelming, but what about the power of gentleness? Can any force defeat a calm and helpful heart? Can a hurricane hurt one's friendliness? Can bloodshed and carnage conquer one's kindness and compassion? Don't the good powers, like benevolence and bigheartedness and generosity, simply smile at evil and carry on with their healing work?

⇥⇤

## UNDER

As I'm writing this, I'm sitting under a ceiling fan set in place years ago by skilled carpenters, under a roof fabricated from good wood and long-lasting shingles, and under a sky as strong and endless as it was billions of years ago. It's a sweltering afternoon, but I'm lucky to be living in a house where I can stand under a shower that flows freely with refreshing water. Outside, I can sit under shade trees that screen me from the sunshine, or under an umbrella that sways in breezes in restful ways. Under me, now and always, is the well-built and reliable earth, and under and around the earth is the universe itself, so sure of its strength and wisdom, so able to stay under and beside us all, assisting us, inspiring us, raising us up.

⇥⇤

## ROUTINE PRECISION

This morning, as I was reading, I noticed that I was stroking the side of my face with my fingers, and, strangely enough, it occurred to me that I was doing it with a certain kind of excellence. I was performing that routine and unremarkable task about as well as it could be done. I sighed and stared out the window for a few seconds, and it seemed like those tasks, too, were done with distinction. I couldn't have sighed and stared any better. Then, as I looked at a small tree outside, I noticed that its small branches were bending in a breeze, and yes, I think they were bending about as perfectly as branches can bend. Putting down my book, I wondered if I could spend the rest of the day just noticing how flawlessly the countless tasks around me are done. Now, hours later,

I'm typing on my laptop keyboard, and my fingers are doing it in a first-class way. Yes, they make mistakes now and then, but even the mistakes are made with matchless precision. I would call them perfect mistakes, errors done with distinction. And just now, I noticed some dust resting on the table beside me – resting, I guess, in precisely the way dust must rest.

# NEWNESS

Like most people, I love the idea of newness, and sometimes it seems to me that there's nothing but newness. Each day I wake to a new morning, a new cup of coffee, and one of Delycia's always-new smiles. All of my thoughts, too, are brand new, though they often look like the same worn-out ones from the past. Each thought actually has a concealed freshness and cleanness, as though my mind is a newly-watered garden or an always-fresh fountain. And of course the grandest newness of all is the matchlessness, the uniqueness, the absolute sparkle of every present moment. I don't usually see that sparkle in the dashing or dawdling kind of day I often have, but it's there, for sure – the lucky flash and shine of right now, right here.

—◄─ ─►—

## NO PROBLEM

I sometimes think I could make good use of the currently popular phrase "no problem". I've had countless problems in my life, problems that seemed to involve all sorts of material difficulties, but whenever I carefully look back at them, it's clear that the "problem" part of them actually existed *only in my thoughts*. I've experienced many unforeseen situations that I didn't understand and hoped could be altered, but this, in itself, does not mean they were problems. A problem, by definition, is a situation that a person *believes* needs to be fought and overcome, and that belief, of course, comes solely from the person's thoughts. If I decide that a situation is my enemy and needs to be defeated, my decision creates the "problem". So, in a sense, I could always say "no problem", because there never are problems "out there" – just situations that need to be accepted, examined, and somehow worked with and perhaps changed. By waging war against situations in my life, I create problems; by welcoming all situations, including so-called "bad" ones, I create open space for myself, and a chance to settle down and let the situations teach me their special lessons.

⊷⊷ ⊶⊶

## UNNOTICED ABUNDANCE

I wonder how much everyday abundance I fail to notice, the way I sometimes absentmindedly pass by the roses overflowing our trellis these days. In my busy comings and goings, I usually don't stop to appreciate the many dozens of pink blossoms spilling over the bars of the trellis, just as I'm sure I heedlessly disregard simple but beautiful lavishness in other places. Stone fences, for instance, are plentiful all along the roads near our house – hundreds of thousands of stones selected for their perfect shapes and shades of gray, and set in place by practiced artisans. It's a lovely bountifulness of natural fencing, but one that I usually pass with hardly a glance. And what about the layers and layers of leaves that are overflowing in trees at this luxurious time of year? Great clouds of leaves softly waver above me, but when do I ever truly notice them, study them,

197

be thankful for them? Above the leaves, too, are sometimes bounteous tiers of clouds that seem to puff their way across the sky, but
when was the last time I really noticed their lushness? When was
the last time I really *looked* at clouds in all their graceful profusion?
This world is a place of pure abundance, and I guess, at 71, it's time
I started seriously noticing it.

=++=

## UNNOTICED SNOWFALLS

Delycia and I have been noticing an almost constant swirling of
small, snow-like particles in the air these early June days, a sort of
springtime storm, a snowfall of blossoms and dust. If we sit with
the sunshine facing us, it's especially noticeable. With a wind blowing, a soft blizzard of white things is spinning across the yard, as
though June has somehow joined up with December. Eating outside, as we often do, we end up with pieces of blossoms and pollen
and who knows what else scattered across our food. What's strange
is that we have to sit in the sunshine in a certain way in order to
see this bizarre pre-summer performance. On cloudy days or if the
sun is to our backs, this June dance is invisible to us, just like, in a
way, the little miracles of life are so often invisible all around me. I
wonder how many unnoticed snowfalls there are -- how many thousands of smiles I don't see, how many cheerless hearts I disregard.

=++=

## A KID AGAIN

I know I'm not really 16, not really a kid with a kid's muscles and
lungs, but I felt like it today as I shoveled snow from our driveway.
The seven inches of snow was almost downy, so it sailed off my
shovel, making the shoveling much easier than I had anticipated. I
felt youthful and frolicsome as I swung the shovel back and forth,

sending great sprays of snow into sizeable hills beside the driveway. I remembered all the cautions about senior citizens straining too much with a snow shovel, so I sometimes paused, rested on my shovel, and savored the snowy scene around me. When I finally finished completely clearing the driveway, I stood silently for a moment, and suddenly I was 16 again, back in Webster Groves, Missouri, surveying a smoothly shoveled driveway before driving out to pick up my date. (I'm actually 72 and, happily, I had a gorgeous girlfriend, age 73, waiting inside with a cup of hot tea.)

⊷ ⊶

## UNRELIABLE – AND RELIABLE – POWER

We lost electric power for a few hours yesterday morning, but we didn't lose the most important power of all, one that's absolutely reliable. All of us have learned by now that electric power is unreliable, likely to leave us powerless at any time for countless haphazard reasons. A gusty storm sweeping through (like yesterday morning's), or a lightning strike, or a faulty transformer – all can cause whole towns to turn temporarily powerless. Yesterday, sirens sounded across town as police and utility workers labored to lead us through several hours of feeling lost without our lights and laptops. Strangely, the outage gave me some time to consider a power that, unlike electricity, is completely dependable. I was thinking of kindness, a power that resists the strongest storms and stays as steady as ever when lightning strikes. Do we ever have to worry about losing the power to be considerate to others? Can the power to be compassionate flicker and fade out like lights? Doesn't it last as long as we wish it to, as long as we understand its power and are open to it? Isn't it always flowing through us, this power to offer our affection in limitless ways to others, and isn't it always able to switch on the lights of unselfishness in our lives? Some of us most likely sat a little stunned in our homes yesterday morning as we wondered what we would do without electric power, but we'll never need to live without the power to be kind. There always abides the undefeated gift of sharing our sympathy and understanding with others, a gift that never stops producing power, even in the severest storms and the wildest lightning.

⊷ ⊶

## BRAKING PERFECTLY

Driving home from the gym one morning, I applied the brakes at a stoplight, and, for some reason, it seemed like I did it perfectly. It felt like I couldn't have braked any better, like I was a first-class user of brakes. I felt like a prizewinner among drivers, a champion of the brake pedal. A few minutes later, I saw a tree limb shake in a wind, and it appeared to shake in a superb way. The shaking somehow had an appearance of refinement and finesse. It seemed like the *crème de la crème* of branch shakings. Then, a few blocks down the road, I made a wrong turn, but – you guessed it – the thought came to me that I made that mistake in a flawless manner. I goofed, but in a great way. It was a blunder, but it seemed to be a beautiful one. Turning into our driveway, I wondered: Is perfection everywhere, if I look carefully enough?

⊷ ⊶

## BRAND NEW SLEEPINESS

When I'm feeling sleepy, really drowsy and heavy-eyed, it sometimes occurs to me, strangely enough, that this sleepiness is brand-new. I think a lot about the simple fact that each moment of my life is completely new, a totally fresh entrance of new sights and sounds and thoughts, and it makes sense, as I think about my drowsiness, that it, too, is always completely new. It is always, you might say, a fresh drowsiness, a clean, unspoiled, up-to-the-minute tiredness.

It's fatigue, but a pristine, mint-condition fatigue. My yawns sometimes seem flawless, just right. My eyelids slowly fall with freshness and sparkle. It's always lethargy of the latest, new-fangled kind.

---

## BREATHING, THINKING, BREATHING
I try to keep in mind that thinking is a lot like breathing. Each day I think and express hundreds of ideas, and I simultaneously listen to and take in other people's ideas. Give out, take in. Give out, take in. My ideas mingle in the air with those of others, much as our breath mingles and mixes all day long. We all breathe in oxygen and breathe out carbon dioxide, and we all give out ideas and take new ideas in. Give out, take in. Give out, take in.

---

## UPHILL AND DOWNHILL
After walking with Delycia this afternoon up and down the small hills in the shoreline village of Noank, it was reassuring to recall the simple fact that for every uphill there's a downhill, and for every struggle there's eventually some sort of peace. I puffed and panted up the hills by the sea, but coming down, I loosened up and felt my breath flowing freely. It was work on the uphill, but almost like amusement on the downhill. This is a little like life, I was thinking later – this cycle of labor followed by leisure, turmoil followed by at least a touch of tranquility. There will always be uphill climbs in my life, and they will always bring sweat and distress, but each will lead, in due course, to fairly free and easy downhill runs and at least a short-lived rest. It's good to know that beyond each of my future mountains will be a break and an easily sloping trail.

---

# HARDIHOOD AND
# GENTLENESS

*"My knights are sworn to vows*
*Of utter hardihood, utter gentleness."*

-Alfred, Lord Tennyson, *"Idylls of the King"*

I have no shining armor and no one calls me a knight, but still, it's easy to see the value in the vows "of utter hardihood [and] utter gentleness" that Tennyson speaks of. At first, the vows may seem contradictory, since hardihood, or strength, might seem the opposite of gentleness, but then I think of the seaport near our house, where the gentle harbor water is strong enough to support schooners and submarines. Also, softly flowing streams are strong enough to slowly dissolve the biggest boulders in their path, which tells me that a gently spirited person can be as brave as a rock-hard warrior. Hardihood is toughness, and true toughness makes use of the power of gentleness. When you're truly gentle, you can join hands with the truly heroic. You can be a secret knight of your neighborhood, a sweet-tempered but forceful fighter for peacefulness.

━━◈ ◈━━

## FEARLESS SENIORS

Yesterday morning Delycia and I enjoyed canoeing on Ninigret Pond, a coastal waterway in Rhode Island, and it brought back an old feeling of being bold, maybe even brave, maybe even a bit rowdy and reckless. Of course, we were on the quietest of salt ponds and were never in any danger, but even so, I felt filled with a strange sense of voyaging and adventure. We were, it sometimes seemed, truly out in the wilds, albeit perfectly civilized wilds, considering the stately summer homes along the shore. At times I imagined that we were paddling frantically to find the next portage in an inhospitable wilderness, conveniently ignoring the fact that all the amenities of a high-class community were a shell's throw away. We wrinkled and worn senior citizens, I said to myself, were valiantly daring to make this dangerous journey, defying colossal odds to make the perilous crossing from Ninigret Park to Fort Ninigret. I thought of us as warrior retirees, fearless seniors, gutsy golden-agers. Nothing could stop us – not winds, not waves, not raspy coughs, not shortness of breath, not old and ramshackle muscles. (Plus, we knew our cell phones were handy, and our car was just a few shell-throws away.)

━━◈ ◈━━

## INSTASPONTANEITY

I'm fairly sure there's no such word as instaspontaneity" so I'm going to invent it, because it's what I see all around me. At any given moment, a great multitude of things are happening instantly and concurrently, sort of like limitless lightning streaks flashing each second. At this particular moment, as I type beside a window, there are trees twisting in the wind, squirrels scooting across the grass, sparrows shaking at the feeders, hearts of wrens and humans holding steady, clouds cruising easily, countless lives being lived with steadiness across the universe – and all of this is instantaneous and synchronized, like an on-the–spot, systematized dance. What's strange is that none of us can avoid being part of this dance. *It's what life is.* Despite being usually unaware of it, I live a totally synchronized, "instaspontaneous" life, flowing ceaselessly and swiftly with all things, from sparrows to spinning planets, in a sudden and well-balanced way.

⊷⊶

### IS THE UNIVERSE TIRED?

I woke up this morning still feeling tired, but then it occurred to me that the universe surely never feels that way – *and I am part of the universe.* If I looked out at the ocean waves on a windy day and saw what seemed to be a separate wave that, for a split second, was smaller than the others, would I say the wave was "tired"? If I saw the wind blowing strongly at one end of our yard but only softly where I was standing, would that mean the soft breeze was "worn out"? If I was standing beside a river and noticed that the current moved more slowly near some debris, would I say the water in that part of the river was "weary"? The universe is an immense creation, and every part of it has a job to do at any particular moment – a job that blends in perfectly with the infinite number of other jobs. No action of the universe is "wide awake" or "tired", "good" or "bad". *It just is.* When I awoke this morning, I put a label on the situation, an old habit of mine. I called it "tired" when I should have just called it "not wanting to get out of bed". Some breezes blow softly, and some people don't jump out of bed in the morning. It's not bad or good. It's just the way the universe works.

≕+ +≕

## WAITING

I've never been good at waiting, but lately it seems easier, especially in these good-natured retirement years. I find I can stop and stay put more often, just letting myself look ahead with interest to what might happen next. I pause more frequently now, and the pauses are somehow instructive for me, small lulls that allow me to actually look at and listen to the everyday life around me. It's easier these days for me to simply linger somewhere, like perhaps at the window to our backyard, just waiting and watching for what the world is ready to reveal – maybe some newly unveiled grass amidst the disappearing snow, maybe March birds sweeping through the air like circus dancers, or maybe just a branch bending slightly in a pre-spring breeze. I wait with willingness now, because I know that whatever happens next will be wonderful in some way, something my customary busyness would surely miss.

≕+ +≕

## HOPING FOR STARS

Yesterday afternoon I found myself hoping the clouds would move off so stars would show at night, but then I thought of other more useful stars, those that always seem to be shining. I have friends, for instance, who somehow find a way to share some light just when I need it, and I can sense their lit-up kindness even when they're far away. Hopeful thoughts, too – even the smallest and slightest – can shimmer like stars, if I stay with them awhile and let their lights illuminate things for me. And then there are spoken words, those most evanescent of all forces, which can create hopeful light in a life faster than almost anything. Happily, I live with someone who sends out words that sparkle like starlit gifts, just when I can most use a little light in my usually lucky life.

⇐✛✛⇒

## WAITING WITH PASSION

I want to become an expert at waiting. I don't mean the kind of waiting that involves being dissatisfied with the present and impatient for something better in the future. No, I want to wait by simply remaining in readiness. I want to be perfectly content to stay in the present moment, quietly watch what happens next, and attentively take pleasure in the mysteries of life as it unfolds. I want to wait by being good-naturedly ready for whatever the universe has prepared for me, and I want to do it in a wholehearted way. I want to wait with enthusiasm for the next surprise, the next revelation, the next miracle, all of which will be constantly appearing, *if* I stay observant. I want waiting to become my pastime and my passion. Instead of always doing and dashing, I want to alertly and eagerly wait. If someone asks me what I do, I want to say, "I wait."

⇐✛✛⇒

# WAKING

Someone asked me recently what time I usually wake up, and I wish I had answered, "Every moment," because, in fact, I *do* awaken each moment, and so does everything and everyone else. This universe, you might say, starts over moment by moment. Each moment is the start of something fresh and up-to-the-minute, the very latest style -- new-fangled, ultramodern, cutting edge. The universe can't help but prepare pristine, unused moments, sort of like an entire organism constantly coming wide-awake – and I am part of all this. Everything's always arousing and stirring, including me. Each moment my blood is newborn, my lungs are cleansed, my countless cells restructured. Each moment a clean, unsullied idea suggests itself to me, like the light of a new star. Awakening is my continuous honor and privilege as a member of this always starting-up universe. Whatever the clock happens to say, that's when I wake up.

## WATCHING MY STEP

"Watch your step" would be a useful slogan for me these days. I especially like the word "watch" because it suggests the kind of completely committed awareness I want to foster in myself – an awareness that sometimes, sadly, seems absent in me for hours and days at a time. I want to be constantly on the alert, attentive as much as possible to the nuances of this oddly beguiling life I'm living. I want to watch what's happening as carefully as a sharp-eyed sailor watches from the deck. This is a demanding mission for me, since a youthful heedlessness still seems more prevalent in me than awareness. I still sometimes see in myself the rash madness of my teenage years. I come panting into a new day, dash through it, and then rush into sleep at the end, hoping that a few hours rest will help me race even faster tomorrow. It's a swift and hassled world we live in, hardly the kind of setting to support "watching your step", but I do want to give it a good try. Instead of simply glancing at the gifts April is giving us along the roads these days, I want to occasionally stop and study them. Instead of quick looks, I want long looks. Instead of just speeding past the songs of birds on my bicycle, I want to truly listen, to sometimes let the bike come to a silent stop among their beautiful songs.

〰〰

## WATCHING THE SHOW

I want to work on watching things more carefully – being a better watcher, you might say, and mostly, I want to watch the workings of my own life. It is, after all, a stirring show, this life I'm lucky to be living. Where it came from, who knows, but just now, at 73, it's still performing with a fair amount of confidence and style on the stage set up for it by the universe. More and more, I want to seat myself in the audience and just watch this strange and occasionally startling show called "The Life of Hamilton Salsich". For a few minutes, now and then, I want to watch the countless thoughts that dance through my mind, swirling their skirts and jackets and singing with finesse their hopeful or forlorn songs. I want to watch the flow of feelings inside me, the way joy sometimes joins with sadness and becomes wisdom, and the way all the feelings seem to flow out of a secret place and then slowly but surely disappear again. I want to watch my silly worries stomping around like they own the stage, and my fears falling over each other as they try to steal the show. It is, indeed, a daring and amusing performance, this life of mine, well worth the price of admission, which is just my willingness to sit still, lighten up, and watch in wonderment.

━━╉╂━━

## WATCHING THE TRAFFIC

Sometimes, at a stop sign in the car or strolling in a city, I simply watch the flow of the traffic, and there's often something strangely serene about it – the sort of disordered evenness of the traffic, the curious turns and swerves it takes, the anomalous stops and start-ups that surprisingly happen in something like smooth routines. It's almost fun to watch it, just as it's sometimes fun to sit off to the side of my mind and watch the movement of a different kind of traffic – the continuous and convoluted flow of my thoughts. Like cars and trucks on highways, my thoughts stream along in a steady and occasionally serpentine manner, sometimes confusing me with their seemingly slapdash patterns, but always and endlessly moving. I see them streaming along -- thoughts of sorrow and happiness, of distress and joyousness, small thoughts and stupendous thoughts – and it's somehow a pleasure to simply observe them as they ceaselessly flow. What's wonderful is the awareness that *they are not me* – that these thoughts are just short-lived cerebral wisps wandering through my life. I can observe them and be mystified by them, but I can also stand back and smile, because *they are not*

209

*me.* The real me stands aside. The thoughts flow by, but "I" stand strongly and peacefully aside.

—&#43;&#43;—

## WATCHING THE TRAIN

Like a never-ending train, thoughts are ceaselessly streaming through my mind, and I would like to learn to simply watch the train rather than climb aboard. What I hope to do, you might say, is stand by the tracks of my mind, or perhaps on a hill above the tracks, and simply observe the thoughts as they pass. Like watching a train back in Missouri when I was a boy, watching my train of thoughts could be a fascinating experience. When a defensive, self-protective thought comes by, I might say, "Wow, look at that bizarre thought!" or, when a happy thought passes, "How did that beautiful thought get made?", or, when an ugly, scary-looking, boxcar kind of thought rumbles by, "That is one hideous thought!" The trick is to just *observe the train, but not jump on board.* So often in my life I have recklessly leaped onto a thought, closed the door, and ridden with it as it careened here and there. Fearful thoughts have taken me on many a riotous ride over the years, as have thoughts of envy, anger, defensiveness, and countless others. *I simply need to refuse to get on the train.* It's much more fun, and far less hazardous, to merely sit on a hillside and watch with fascination as the endless train of thoughts harmlessly and safely passes by.

—&#43;&#43;—

## GIVING BY SURRENDERING

As I was watching the wind in the trees beside our house yesterday afternoon, and the trees swaying and sort of surrendering to the wind, it seemed to me they were giving a gift to the wind – giving their loose-limbed suppleness so the wind could work its way through them with ease. It started me wondering if surrendering is, indeed, sometimes like giving, which is perhaps why we use "give in" and "give up" as synonyms. If a serious snowstorm hits, I can simply give in, or surrender, to it, which might mean giving my acceptance, even my approval, to the storm, and just sitting back and taking some pleasure in its magnificence. Likewise, if I take on a task and things don't go precisely my way, I can surrender to the task by giving up my self-assured stubbornness, thus freeing my mind to find new ways to do the work. Of course, surrendering could also be simply a way of ducking a difficult situation, but there are situations, surely, where surrendering could actually be a way of giving, or giving back, to life itself – giving my willingness to it, my acceptance of it, my readiness to do whatever needs to be done to welcome its richness. Perhaps I can learn to be as limber and yielding as trees, and just bend and lean with life instead of opposing it.

---

## WEIGHING THOUGHTS

Many people make a habit of weighing themselves each day, but I wonder if we shouldn't weigh our thoughts as well. After all, thoughts can exert power over our lives, and wouldn't it be helpful to have some knowledge of which thoughts weighed so much that they could bully and browbeat us, and which were as weightless as the wind? Wouldn't it be nice to know that a thought was so insubstantial that it was as harmless as a passing puff of spring air? Some thoughts, though, can create a great weight in our lives, almost like a load we carry and call our own, and "weighing" those thoughts – seeing just how much influence they wield with us – can alert us to their power and cause us to carefully set them down and smile and walk away. I can picture myself in the morning, taking the time to weigh a few thoughts, then setting the heavy ones in the wastebasket and watching the light ones waft around me and drift off while others float up from far away.

※⊹⊹※

## WHAT DO YOU SEE?

It's a simple truth that I can choose what I see in any situation. In a storm, I can see cause for concern and stress, or I can see nature's abiding magnificence. In serious illness, I can see hopelessness, or I can see a chance, once again, to choose buoyancy and brightness over gloom. In failure, I can see defeat, or I can see a fresh start. At 3:00 a.m., I can see sleepless darkness, or I can see sunrise just ahead.

※⊹⊹※

## WHAT HAPPENED TO THE PAIN?

I injured my shoulder a few days ago (playing kickball with my grandchildren), but today for an hour around noon there was no pain and no problem, for I was dancing with absolute rowdiness with Delycia and a few dozen other upstart, audacious dancers. This was the "noon dance" at a retreat center – sixty minutes of madness and freedom and forgetfulness of troubles for one and all. We were led by a warmhearted teacher who taught us, slowly and easily, to simply let go and take pleasure in our ability to move. Before too many minutes had passed, we were prancing and sway-ing here and there, throwing ourselves around among strangers of all shapes and ages. I swirled past people who, perhaps, were suffering from secret griefs of all kinds, and yet only smiles could be seen. Overweight or willowy, we forgot our sorrows (and sore shoulders) and lost ourselves, for an hour or so, in the joy of jump-ing and skipping like young, high-spirited, dancers.

※⊹⊹※

# WHAT I NEED

I sometimes slip into my old practice of listing things I need – another shirt, some better boots, more stamina when working out – but the truth is that something bigger than me makes a much better list. Call it God, or the Universe, or Life, or just Inspiration – there's a power, I sense, that sees what I need and somehow supplies it. When I occasionally get my busybody self out of the way, and just listen to what this wiser power is saying to me, the things I really need (not just want) seem to unmistakably shine in my thoughts. This morning, for instance, when I was doing some of this silent listening, it became obvious that I didn't actually need another shirt, but instead, perhaps I needed just that moment of silence during which I was seeing clearly the birds breakfasting at the feeder. When I set aside my persistent and restless ego, and simply listen to this soft but measureless voice from somewhere, I sometimes understand that all I really need is the revitalized blood my good heart is constantly giving me and the thoroughly new thoughts my mind is always making. I sometimes see that this particular moment – any moment – is all I really ever need.

—⊷ ⊶—

## WHAT IT'S ABOUT

If I wanted to write the story of my life (which I don't), the strange fact is that it wouldn't be about me. It wouldn't be about some separate person named Hamilton who has been at the center of countless separate, personal experiences, as though I am the main character in a decades-long drama about myself. Life isn't like that – isn't separate and disconnected and personal. Life – anyone's life – is a measureless sea, of which the "person" is simply one of countless essential, infinitesimal currents. My life story would not be about a separate "me", but about the endless sea of life that has swirled and flowed across the universe in the years from 1941 to now. I am simply an ever-rolling ripple in this sea, and my story, like anyone's, would be the story of the whole and never-ending sea itself. If someone asked me what my life is about, I would say it's not about me, but about all the mornings and midnights since 1941, and about all the winds and seasons, and all the friends and families across the earth, and all the forlorn and friendless people everywhere, and all the trees and blossoms, and the spinning earth and all the stars and planets and the old, astonishing universe. That's what my life's about.

—⊷ ⊶—

## WHATEVER THINGS ARE USEFUL

Thousands of thoughts pass across my mind each day, and over the years, I've grown more and more determined to entertain, as often as possible, only the most useful ones. If I have a choice in the matter – and I always do – why would I choose to play host to an unpleasant thought when so many pleasing ones are waiting to bolster and inspire me? Why would I choose to linger with a gloomy thought when countless heartening thoughts are standing by? I'm not suggesting a pollyanna approach to living, just a sensible one. I will occasionally face stressful situations, of course, but I can do it most successfully with thoughts that are constructive rather than despairing, thoughts that show the way forward rather than the way down, thoughts that clarify rather then confuse. If someone set before me a ten dollar bill and a one, I'd choose the ten in a flash, and I'll pick a bright thought over a dark one any day.

⸺✦✦⸺

## ELEGANT DEATHS

"When the leaves fall, the whole earth is a cemetery pleasant to walk in."

-- Henry David Thoreau, "Autumn Tints"

Death does its busiest work in the autumn, and yet no one sheds a tear as the colorful leaves flutter to the ground. The vivid leaves that fall to our lawns have all died, and yet there are no cries of sorrow among us, no sounds of grief and bereavement. In fact, autumn is more often a time of celebration, a time when kids kick up leaves with laughter and cider is shared around tables with pleasure. It's strange that the silent, serene death of these countless leaves usually leaves us appreciative rather than sad, satisfied rather than sorrowful. Perhaps it's because the leaves die in such peace, and with such gracefulness. They don't appear to fight their fall and their end, but seem to float with it in a kind of relaxed reverie, as if they know their deaths will result in the rise of fresh new life. When my time comes, I hope I can meet it with as much poise and deportment as our Mystic autumn leaves.

—◁+ +▷—

## WHITE LIGHT

Driving with Delycia on country roads this overcast morning, it began to seem like there was a great light almost everywhere, and that it came from the snow-covered fields. The sky was gray, but the widespread fields seemed full of white light, as though something was shining just under the snow. It even seemed to me that the grayness of the sky was actually some sort of softer light sent up from the white snow. Before long, the overcast day seemed like a bright one, a day when old, resting snow did all the shining.

—◁+ +▷—

## WHITE WORK

Sometimes, as my wife and I sleep in our bedroom, a humidifier quietly creates what is called white noise, and every night and every day the dependable universe produces a steady stream of what I might call "white work". It's work that wants to stay secret and silent, softly behind the scenes, work that discreetly does what must be done to keep things always spinning and expanding and advancing. It's the work my body, for instance, calmly carries out moment by moment – the balanced moving of blood, the perfect falling and lifting of the lungs, the constant re-creation of cells. It's the silent work the surrounding air always does, sending me breezes and brand-new oxygen and always a feeling of freshness. And then there's the endless "white work" of the wide world I live in – the rolling along of rivers, the constant progress of winds that work their way without ceasing across thousands of miles, and of course the noiseless, steadfast spinning of the stars. It's reassuring to me to stay aware of this "white work" – to realize, while I'm working my way through the minutes of a day, that so much silent work is always being done inside and around me, that so much steady and gentle effort is being quietly made to make my life this marvelous thing that it is.

⋙✦⋘

## WHO SENT ME?

Today, as I was running some errands for myself, this thought came to me: Who sent me? Who sent me to the gift shop and Staples? Where did this thought of doing these errands come from? Who sent me? Pretty quickly, as I thought about it, I realized that I'm sent somewhere almost every second of the day. One thought sends me to the teapot, then another thought sends me to stir my omelet, then another sends me to the table to set out some napkins for Delycia and me. It's as if these thoughts are standing beside me, pointing to particular places and whispering their instructions. Sometimes I'm sent to see if there's a fancy sunset over the Mystic River. Sometimes I'm sent to give my wife a quiet kiss. Somewhere, there's a sender that's doing all this, and I'm grateful to it. Some might call it God, or Allah, or the Tao, or perhaps just the endless universe that somehow sent us all here in the first place.

⋙✦⋘

## TOUCHED

It's wonderful that we can so often be touched by the world around us – touched by even the smallest flowers or faraway stars in the sky. Of course I'm thinking here of the non-physical kind of touching, the kind that causes us to say "I was touched by what he said" or "Her performance was very touching." We can be touched, in that sense, by the forlorn look on a face, or by a few beautiful words in a sentence, or simply by the rise and fall of a grief-stricken friend's voice. It's an invisible kind of touching, like unseen fingers pressing softly on our souls for a few seconds. Recently I gathered with a group of good friends, and I was deeply touched by their sorrowful but brave approach to some unfortunate news they had heard about a colleague. Their sorrow touched me, but so did their courage and wisdom. Their words were like hands held out to each other in solidarity, and I was touched by their sense of fellowship. Their thoughts and feelings were not physical, but they filled the room – and touched me – in an unforgettable way.

## PLENTY OF ROOM INSIDE

Over the years, it has occasionally seemed that I simply couldn't handle any more difficulties, almost as though my life was a somewhat small room that could contain only so many troubles. I'm not sure where that thought came from – that belief that my inner spirit is a compact and cramped place – but as the years have passed I have come to see it as far from the truth. My inner spirit, my "heart and soul", like all of ours, is vast beyond measure. There are no walls to someone's inner being, no boundaries to a person's thoughts and feelings and vivacity and passion. The inner spirit that all of us have can spread itself out across infinite distances inside us. There's endless room in all of us for compassion and patience and love and lightheartedness that can last forever. There's boundless space in our hearts and souls, both for all the blessings of life *and* for all its countless disappointments. As difficulties arise in my life, I simply need to say, as I do when success shows up, "Come on in. There's plenty of room."

# WINGS, WINDS, THOUGHTS

A s we sat at breakfast this morning in the sunroom, great
groups of birds were storming our feeders or sitting silently
on the bushes below them, hoping for a shot at some seeds, but
every so often, they would all rush off with a furious flap of wings.
If you weren't looking, it almost sounded like a sudden wind, as if
a small storm had swiftly passed. It called to mind the moments of
my life, usually the stirring ones, that seem to quickly come and
go, those short-lived seconds of excitement that burst up as if on
wings. I can be calm and commonplace, resting in the center of my
familiar life, when suddenly I'm flying off with some free-wheeling
thoughts. Where these wild flocks of thoughts come from, I have
no idea, and neither do I know where the sea of sparrows and
finches swept in from this morning. There's a mystery about where
these surprises came from, just as there's a mystery about where
love comes from, or goodness, or sincerity, or the power to "be
there" when a friend's life falls apart. We can be sitting in silence
after supper, and suddenly we feel the great force of kindness filling us, or we're swept away on the wings of wanting to make the

world better. With thoughts like these it can happen that suddenly, like the throng of birds breaking away from the feeder in a swift and wonderful flurry.

＝≒ ≒＝

## WINTER GIFTS

Today's hard-blowing blizzard has me thinking of the gifts winter gives us. Sure, there are hardships associated with today's storm, but I'm trying to see its gifts more than its adversities. There's the gift of the fluffy, flying snow – a sight that still thrills me like it did when I was a boy. Someone who had never seen snow would be astonished at what I see outside my window just now – an endless dance of soft white pieces of enchantment, a gift to make an old guy get young again. Then there are the gifts given by the strong wind -- the flowing, multifarious snowdrifts, as distinctive as sculptures in a gallery. Tomorrow, I will tour the snow gallery in our neighborhood, admiring these once-in-a-lifetime snow sculptures produced by this gift-giving storm. I may feel more fortunate than ever as I look at what the storm – now vanished into the universe – produced for me.

＝≒ ≒＝

## WISDOM SPEAKING

Like all of us, I occasionally pick up some new knowledge -- even what I might call wisdom -- here and there, but actually, a very high kind of wisdom speaks to me, and all of us, all day long. Unfortunately, I am often too frazzled with forty different things on my mind to listen to these quiet calls of wisdom (or Wisdom, since it's everywhere) – these soft voices of understanding that signal me from both far inside and far away. It takes stillness to hear what Wisdom is saying. It takes settling down and setting aside the countless concerns I carry with me, and then absolutely listening to what this wise force in my life is saying to me.

⊷⊹⊹⊶

## WISDOM

I sometimes wonder if gaining wisdom isn't as hard as I've thought. Perhaps it's like simply opening my inner eyes and looking through the very wide windows inside me. The problem is that there seem to be countless other windows inside me, as well – tiny, narrow ones – and I spend most of my time squinting through those, always seeing only obstacles and endless mazes. Perhaps wisdom, at least a passing sample of it, comes when we turn to the wide windows, the endlessly wide ones, and see the truly vast panorama of reality. The scenery of my life sometimes seems surrounded by borders and restrictions, as though I'm living in a small and mystifying maze, but wisdom occasionally wakes me up, and then I can look through its spacious windows and see how immeasurable my life and all lives really are. It's like suddenly standing on the summit of Mt. Everest and seeing reality, all of it, spread out in endless vistas below me. That's what wisdom does when I simply look through the right windows.

⊷⊹⊹⊶

## NEVER BY MYSELF

I sometimes like to think I'm doing something "by myself", when the truth is that it's an impossibility. I am never truly by myself, never a totally solitary, separate person. I am an intertwined piece of a thoroughly unified universe, and as such I am inseparably linked with countless other persons and things. In a sense, thousands of "friends" are with me every second. All the people I've ever known, for instance, are still with me, since their influence, no matter how slight, is still inside me somewhere, still assisting me in making decisions. Also, the air around me is with me, joined to me at all times, continuously flowing into my lungs in a helpful way. And even on overcast days, some sort of sunlight is constantly with me, lighting my way, lending a helping hand. The list of my "assistants" goes on and on: the cells in my body that work ceaselessly to support my endeavors; the blood that brings newness so I know what to do next; the heart that's always right there with me, pumping with perfection like a partner. I might sometimes pretend that I'm "by myself", but the truth is that untold "friends" are ever with me, making living a rather exciting and cordial collaboration.

## NEW MOMENT, NEW FACE?

Every so often, it becomes clear to me that each moment is a brand new one, never before seen or experienced in the whole history of the universe. Try as I may, I can't imagine anything in any present moment that's not completely unused and fresh. Moments may *seem* to contain odds and ends from the past, but those odds and ends are all experienced in the brand new moment called Now. If I say, staring at the mirror, that my face is surely not new, the statement itself is said in the pristine present moment. The statement is about "oldness", but the statement, as well as the thought behind it and the moment itself, shines with sheer newness. I can label my face, with all its furrows and grooves, as "old", but since it's staring back at me in a totally new and unspoiled moment, it must somehow share in that unblemished newness. As strange as it may sound, if the moment is new, must not the face also be new? *I wonder* . . . Could thinking this way – thinking about the absolute inescapability of newness – actually transform the appearance of a face? Could my well-wrinkled face, seen in the mirror always with a spirit of newness, slowly seem somewhat newer, day by day?

—⊰+⊱—

## WITH EACH OTHER

It's strange that most of us see ourselves, at least sometimes, as basically separate and alone in this life – strange, because togetherness is perhaps the most fundamental truth about the universe. We *can't* be alone, even if we wanted to, for all of life is linked in innumerable and unbreakable ways. To take a simple example, when I see people passing by on the street, they live, if briefly, inside me, in my eyesight and my thoughts. They have their own private lives, but those lives are linked to mine because I carry them, for a few seconds, inside me. We are, in a sense, side by side in our lives as we pass along the street. We share this world in special but unseen ways – by breathing the same air as we pass, by seeing the same sunlight and feeling the same air flowing past us, by placing our feet down on the same trustworthy planet as we walk. Even our feelings are shared among us, for who can keep a feeling from flowing out to everyone? A feeling, be it love or loneliness, cannot be kept inside us like locked boxes, since all feelings flow among all people like the sea washes the shores of its countless islands. If I'm sad, I'm simply sharing in the boundless sadness of the world, and any happiness that happens to pass through me is the same happiness that lifts up lives in Indonesia and Indianapolis. We dwell in endless alliances, whether we know it or not. We are comrades and collaborators, created by the same extraordinary universe and seeking, side by side, the same happiness that heals us all.

—⊰+⊱—

# WONDERS IN THE LAND OF HAM

Browsing through the Bible recently, I was surprised to come upon this phrase in Psalm 106: "... the wonders in the land of Ham". I'm sure I nodded and smiled, since I'm often called Ham, and since the land of my life is definitely full of wonders. Like all of us, I have a fair share of struggles, but they are easily outweighed by the wonders. To me, it's a wonder that blood brings fresh energy to my body moment by moment, and that my lungs repeatedly lift with new life. As I write this, I'm amazed that I'm partaking in the full-of-wonders process of being part of this universe, a process that started and continues with no help from me. As I sit with my laptop in the shade on this summer day, wonders work their magic all around me – tree limbs turning almost tenderly in a wind, a leaf falling to the grass with gracefulness, a sky carrying clouds no one has ever seen before. Yes, in the land of Ham (Salsich), each second brings a surprise, and each day makes way more wonders than struggles.

⊷╬ ╬⊶

## WORDS AND CLASSROOMS

"In the beginning was the word" is a Bible phrase that always seemed strangely associated with my duties as a teacher, and today, as my former colleagues look forward to launching a new school year tomorrow, I'm thinking of how lucky they will be to feel the force of words in their classrooms. I guess we could say that words stand at the beginning of all things in classrooms. All lessons, exercises, readings, writings, quizzes, tests, all discussions, debates, arguments, speeches, lectures, comments, and remarks start with the force of a few words. Even the thousands of thoughts that arise during a given class period are constructed with words, as buildings are built with boards and stones and steel. Words are a sort of camouflaged force in the classroom, a force that kindles thoughts and carries conversations, a force that stands ready at the starting line of everything teachers and their students do. In fact, it has always seemed to me – and I often shared this with my students – that students and teachers do business with the strongest power in the universe. All wars start with words, as do all friendships, adventures, transformations, and triumphs. A world without words is a garden without daylight, a seed without soil. I'm grateful that I found myself, for 45 years, surrounded in the classroom by the everlasting liveliness of words, and tomorrow I'll think happily of the teachers in my former school as they and their students set forth on another educational mission, with the steadfast assistance of spirited and inspiring words.

⊱⊰

## WORDS AND WIND

Sometimes it seems like I'm just wasting words when I'm letting them loose lickety-split in a conversation, but when I recall how the wind works, I usually relax and listen with pleasure as the words pass among us. As the wind blows back and forth and here and there with full freedom, all its movements make something special happen, even if I don't notice it, and perhaps all my words work some sort of magic in their secret way. Perhaps I should always speak with enthusiasm, simply because I'm sending out the special powers of thoughts, like the wind lets loose its helpful forces across the earth. The wind never makes a mistake as it makes its way among us, and maybe our words, as long as they're spoken sincerely and without spite, always stir up something helpful for our lives. It could be that I should share my words more willingly and freely, sending them forth with a kind of confident enthusiasm, simply throwing my thoughts out like seeds to see what springs up. Could I speak like the wind works, with flexibility, free rein, and some type of gracefulness -- a force, one way or another, for good?

## WORDS ARE LIFE

Delycia and I saw the movie "The Book Thief" this afternoon, and, in the midst of our sighs and silent tears, I think we both saw something very special in this film. I was particularly struck by this phrase, said by one of the characters: "Words are life." Indeed, I thought, words *are* life -- and love and goodness and strength and everything else. Words work wonders every hour, every moment, all across the earth. Words start all friendships and all fights. Without words, there would be neither love affairs nor wars. Words are like diamonds and bombs, like coats to keeps us warm and ropes to whip us with. In a great book, it says that in the beginning was the word, meaning, maybe, that at the start of everything, words wait with their mighty power. In the film, Liesel Meminger understands this, and therefore steals books in order to come into contact with this power. She touches her books like they're time bombs, which, for those of us who love them, they are.

## SMILING AT WRINKLES

Since I feel rather fond of mine, it's strange to me that so many senior citizens seem to hate their skin's wrinkles. After all, wrinkles in the skin show that a person has survived for scores of years – has made a good fight of it, has stayed strong through decades, has done what needed to be done to enter the eminent empire of old age. Wrinkles mean perseverance, stamina, staying power. In some parts of the world, people with the most wrinkles receive the most reverence, simply because they've endured and carried on – and also because others sense that wisdom silently spreads out from these creased and craggy senior citizens. I'm not sure how much wisdom my old furrowed head contains, but I do smile when I see my wrinkles in the mirror. I give a silent shout of thankfulness that life has given me all these ridges and grooves, all these wrinkly badges of honor, all these crumpled emblems of a long and lucky life.

⇥ ⇤

## WRITING LIKE A HOLIDAY

The artist Paul Klee once said that art should be like a holiday - something to give the artist the opportunity to see things differently and to change her or his point of view – and I have gradually grown to feel the same about writing. Now, in my 72nd year, when I sit with my laptop and start tapping the keys, it's as if I've set out on a holiday escapade, as if restrictions have been rescinded and boundaries broken down. The words seem to lead the way, and I just cheerfully follow along to see what surprises will show up. These days, when I begin writing, it's like I'm leaving behind rules and strategies and boundaries, and simply wandering in a boundless land. Writing for me has become a sort of free-wheeling adventure, a time to celebrate the unlimited freedom of thought that all of us possess, a time to revel and carouse with phrases and sentences to see what wonders might arise. It's my daily holiday in retirement, a vacation in the wide-ranging kingdom of words.

⟨⟩

## YEAH, NO

It's strangely inspiring to hear people say "yeah, no" so often these days, as in "Yeah, no, I think it's a great idea." I guess it reminds me, in a funny way, of the fundamental truth that life is made of opposites. Yeah, life's superb, but no, it can also be dismal. Yeah, it's a blessing, but no, it's sometimes a catastrophe. Yeah, there's May's brightness, but no, there's December's blizzards. To me, it speaks of the overall fairness of life, its evenhandedness, its insistence on a little bit of this and a little bit of that. Life's like a dance: yeah, a sway to the left, no, a swing to the right; yeah, a twirl, no, a swirl. It's this secret, ever-present balance in all things that lets the universe surge up and down, right and left, with perfect poise. My task is to see and appreciate this poise, this overall constancy, this gift of the general evenness of all of life. Yeah, no, there's darkness, but also lots of light.

⟨⟩

## YIELDING

Sometimes, when I see a "YIELD" sign on an entrance to an Interstate, I smile with reassurance, for it reminds me that I can constantly yield to the bountiful power that runs all things. I'm not talking about God, at least not the God that gave me fits all through my childhood – the God that could crush me in anger as easily as bless me. No, the power that I can continuously yield to is simply the force that flows through this spirited universe, the force that both thinks all my thoughts and throws the starlight across the sky each night. It's the force that's forever doing all the jobs that I usually mistakenly think I'm responsible for, everything from lifting and lowering my lungs to making sure I'm safe in stressful circumstances. It's the power that pushes summer winds through fulsome trees and places feelings of all kinds inside me. It tells me to turn left or stare at a stunning sunset. It leads me, and therefore lets me love my life rather than worry about it. However, I have to have the good sense to yield to this power, to let it freely flow like the traffic on I-95, like the blood that streams through my body without any help from me.

# A GRATUITOUS LIFE

I t often amazes me to realize how gratuitous my life has been – how totally unearned and unmerited most of the gifts I've received have been. Yes, I know I've occasionally worked hard and earned some justifiable rewards, but the big gifts, the important gifts, have come to me as unearned, free-of-charge bestowals. There's the flood of helpful thoughts that flow through me each day, all of them coming without much effort on my part. I don't strain and sweat to make useful thoughts; they somehow simply show up, like on-the-house gifts from the universe. And what did I do to deserve being born of hard-working, level-headed, and loving parents? I showed up in November of 1941, and there before me was the unearned gift of a well-off, wonderful family. Finally, there are the gifts I get day by day – a smile from someone, or a sweet word of kindness, or hours of steady sunshine, all handed to me on a platter free of charge. Should I feel embarrassed about all these handouts, or just grateful for a universe that seems to give because it's fun?

## A HOLY BACKYARD

I recall that somewhere in the Bible the phrase "a holy place " is used, and I thought of it today as I was sitting beside Delycia in our backyard surrounded by her overflowing flower gardens. I hope I don't offend anyone when I say that our backyard seems as holy a place as any church. Don't we go to church to worship what's beautiful and good and true, and don't I find that in our backyard on a daily basis? What's more beautiful than a crowd of lustrous coreopsis blossoms, and what's more full of goodness than grand trees sharing their shade on a summer day? And where is the truth, and the whole truth, better found than in an everyday backyard with breezes blowing by and birds swooping and singing all around? I agree with Emily Dickinson, who said she kept the Sabbath by staying at home and listening in her garden to the sermons of God, "a noted Clergyman". What better sermon than the sight of feverfew blossoms floating on their stems, or the sound of house wrens having dignified discussions beside their nest?

＝┿ ┿═

## A TIP OF THE HAT

During a walk with Delycia on this warm morning, I took my hat off whenever we entered a shady area, just to cool down, and it started me thinking about the old custom of men "tipping their hats", and perhaps bowing with stately graciousness, when in the presence of someone special. We weren't walking past kings and queens this morning, but we were surely in the midst of magnificence. There were, for instance, majestic old trees along the streets, some of which were here when my grandparents were young, and which still stand in a resplendent and regal way. Do they not deserve a tip of the hat and a bow? And what about the soft winds that cooled us as we walked, winds that have been working their magic in a solemn and measured manner for eons? Shouldn't an old, grateful guy occasionally give them a tip of the hat and a cultured bow as he walks in the morning with his sweetheart?

⊶ ⊷

## BUT

"But" is a simple, unfussy word that sometimes helps me stay humble. When I think I clearly understand something, the word "but" occasionally steps in to show me what I missed. If I say some situation is just what I need, "but" says there are elements in it that I definitely don't need, as in "You love these fresh cherries, but you don't need to eat dozens of them." If I say sorrow has nothing good in it for me, "but" shows me some understanding I can gain from it, as in, "Your loss has brought you sadness, but watch for the wisdom that waits inside it." The word "but" scolds me in kindhearted ways: "You think you're right in this argument, but you see only a small sliver of the truth." "You think you know what you need, but that's like saying you know what the Grand Canyon needs." "You think you know yourself, but yourself is like thousands of miles of wilderness mountains."

⊶ ⊷

## GENTLE PRESENCE

Like most of us, I have known some people who inspired me by just their gentle presence, their facility for somehow spreading mellowness around simply by being present. They don't necessarily "do" anything – don't speak about gentleness or show off their calmness or even seem particularly peaceful. They simply spread out gentleness the way a soft summer day spreads out warmth. These people carry kindness with them like a light that constantly shines. Their understanding seems immeasurable, as if nothing can disturb it, and their compassion comes with a feeling of vastness and serenity. They bring the sweet-temperedness of a soft shift in the weather, sunshine after days of clouds. When they're with us, their presence alone brings mildness and mercy.

＝⊱ ⊰＝

## GETTING HELP FROM THE UNIVERSE

I love to recall a day when I put together a large garden cart for my wife. It was an inspiring experience, because I saw, a short time after I started, that I was receiving substantial help from something so large and wise it's like a limitless mind – the universe itself. I realized, once again, that I am an inseparable part of this universe – a small speck, yes, but one that's absolutely blended with the vast universe that started me off some 70+ years ago. The stars and winds are as much in me as I am in then. The atoms that sweep in and out of me make the sun shine as effortlessly as they make my bones and blood brand new each moment. The fragments that form my body were born at the Big Bang as surely as some of the galaxies were. As I was stumbling through the instructions for assembling the cart, for some reason I thought of the stars and how stalwart they are, and somehow I felt their spreading strength inside my mind. If they can shine so effortlessly for eons, perhaps I could construct this cart with stylish smoothness as well. If the winds could efficiently work their sorcery across thousands of miles, then maybe I could make this garden gift for my wife come together with easiness and satisfaction. Surprisingly, several hours later we were both looking at a smartly finished garden cart that can carry compost and leaves for years to come.

＝⊱ ⊰＝

## THE BEAUTY AND POWER OF INTERRUPTIONS

This morning the pastor of the church we've been occasionally attending gave an inspiring sermon on the beauty and power of interruptions. She helped me see that my life, and all of life, is, surprisingly, a steady stream of interruptions, and that all of these interruptions are actually a part of the affirmative and healthful flow of the universe through us. (She used the word "God", but I sometimes use "the universe", to remind me that God is not a person.) An interruption is like the universe knocking on yet another door to show us still more miracles, and perhaps the best way to respond is to just smile and open the door. Curiously, the word "interruption" derives from the Latin "rumpere", meaning "to break", suggesting that an interruption could be seen as the universe breaking through to show me something special, or even breaking me open like a bud breaks into blossoms. Already today I have experienced hundreds of these moment-by-moment interruptions, small side streams that flowed into and refurbished my life. I hope I've smiled and welcomed them and asked what they could show me.

# PERMITTING THE FLOW

The word "permit" derives from two Latin words meaning "flow through", which makes me realize that I should do a lot more permitting in my life. I especially need to permit thoughts and situations to flow through my life as effortlessly as they naturally want to do. Thoughts and situations, after all, are not stationary objects, but ever-moving events in the endless procession called life. They come to us, but with surprising speed they always go from us, passing away and usually leaving just a mist in the memory. My problem is that I often don't permit my thoughts and situations to flow in their effortless, inexorable way. Strangely enough, I seem to set up barriers, so that thoughts and situations, especially the worrisome ones, are blocked from flowing through, and instead, stay solid and real in my life for far too long. I need to remember that everything passes away soon enough, including thoughts and situations. I should probably sit more often on the bank of the river of my life and give it permission to flow easily by.

## TREASURE AT HOME

I was recalling today the old fairy tale about the guy who leaves home for many years to search for treasure, only to return home to find it buried in his own yard. We've all done our share of searching for the "treasure" called contentment, and, in the end, don't we occasionally realize that the contentment we were seeking was somehow beside us all the while? I have a feeling that the present moment – any present moment – is a treasure box of contentment, but sadly, I rarely recognize it. Most moments in a day, I'm off on the great search for ease and satisfaction, perhaps in several more lemon cookies, perhaps in purchases of things I don't need, perhaps in daydreams about maybe's and what if's. Occasionally, though, I do return, sometimes exhausted, to the present moment, which is always right here for me, always loyal, always waiting with its treasures. Every moment is a chest of riches, and it's not even buried, except to folks like me who have good eyes but sometimes can't see.

## DIVERSIFIED TURF

I often tell Delycia how fond I am of the variety of flowers she has surrounded us with in her gardens, and lately I've been feeling just as fortunate to have a richly varied lawn. I suppose we have some ordinary "grass" growing in the lawn, but we also have a bountiful profusion of what some people would call weeds, but what I'm now calling "diversified turf". I am proud to present to visitors a lawn filled, not just with ordinary, nondescript grass, but with exotic green growths like curlydock, buckhorn plantain, common cinquefoil, creeping oxalis, ground ivy, and moss-eared chickweed. Yes, some people would call these weeds, but after all, "weeds" is just a word. When I see our sundry and special lawn filled with such prosperous greenery as sheep sorrel, white clover, and dandelion, I don't say "weeds". I say "diversified turf" and take a stand for all things green.

---

## A 74-YEAR-OLD CLOUD

As I was watching some clouds carrying themselves across the sky today and slowly shifting their shapes, it occurred to me that I am a sort of cloud myself. I, too, am constantly changing, despite my deceptively fixed appearance. If people had seen me sitting outside this afternoon, they wouldn't have seen the river of fresh thoughts flowing through me, each one new and special, each one making me someone slightly new. Nor would they have seen the cells in my body being purified or replaced, or the fresh oxygen bringing newness to my lungs, or the blood ferrying freshness to every part of my body. They would have seen a 74-year-old silvery guy staring at the sky, perhaps at a fluffy cloud that first looked like a lion, then a ship, then a sailing heart. They wouldn't have noticed that his life was slightly new each moment. They wouldn't have seen what was constantly being born inside him.

---

## A LARGER LIFE

Slowly it has become clear to me that my little life, the one I've been carefully protecting all these years, is not little at all and does not need my protection. Decades ago, as a boy, I somehow became convinced that what I called "my" life was a small, separate, and at-risk entity, but now I see how mistaken I was. I see that "my" life is not mine at all, but is part of, and belongs to, the endless universe, the way a drop of water belongs to the ocean or a wisp of a breeze belongs to the everlasting wind. I see that I no more need protection than does a drop of ocean water. The drop drifts with its vast ocean, the breeze works within the wind, and I move as the universe moves, swirling along with the currents of life the way stars stream along in the immensity of the sky. I do sometimes like to pretend that I, by myself, perform and produce, but I know now that it's the endless universe (some people call it "God") that always does the work. I see I am part of something so large it makes "my" artificial little life, the one I invented in boyhood and have been caring for ever since, seem utterly fictitious and silly.

⊷⊶

## LIFE IN THE AUDIENCE

It seems fitting that in these, my retirement years, I have decided to formally retire from my role as a performer. In a way, I have been performing on a daily basis for most of my life, trying my best to do countless big and little jobs as perfectly as possible. I guess I felt I had to "prove something" over and over by carrying out this or that duty in a successful manner. It was as though I was on stage, and only the best performance would earn applause. *No more, though.* I've stepped down from the stage and am now sitting serenely in the audience, watching the wonderful world I live in perform. Just now the sky above me is doing its "light blue with wispy cloud" performance, a breeze is executing its "brushing against flowers" routine, sparrows are showing off their flits and flutters at the feeders, my lungs are doing their lifting and falling presentation in a perfect way, and even the distant traffic on the interstate is staging its own show of smooth and steady sounds. Tell me, why should I bother to perform when there's so much to see on the stage of this surprising world?

⊷⊶

## TO THE HARBOR

A friend who has been feeling the effects of a long-standing physical problem told me recently that he now sees that the problem is like a wind that's actually "bringing [him] home to the harbor" (his words). He said that somehow this physical difficulty is slowly blessing him with a greater awareness that his real home is actually the entire vast universe, and not his small, sometimes distressed body. He said this chronic problem seems to have opened him to what he called "the immensity of life itself", and he knows, now, that he's part of an immeasurable "wind" that's softly and irresistibly blowing toward greater understanding. He said he has come to think of his physical discomfort as an opportunity. (He explained that the word "opportunity" derives from Latin words meaning "in the direction of the harbor".) He said he certainly doesn't welcome or enjoy the discomfort, but he's watching it patiently and earnestly to see how it takes him to a harbor, and how some new understanding slowly spreads out on the horizon.

# ROOMY HEARTS

Recently, as I was thinking about an old hymn that says a grateful heart is one that has ample "room", it occurred to me that a heart has more than ample room in it. In its true state, my "heart" -- meaning my inner spirit – has no walls, no boundaries, no limits of any kind. My heart can hold as much as life can produce – all the heartbreaks, sorrows, and disappointments, as well as all the joys and delights. If I could imagine a house whose walls and ceiling extend out for an infinite distance, that's the kind of room my inner spirit actually has. What produces this endless roominess is the simple fact that my inner life – my "heart" – is not made of a material substance, and thus doesn't have borders and fences or beginnings and endings. My true heart, like all of ours, is made of spirit, not matter, and therefore has a spaciousness that defies measurement. It can easily expand to make room for anything that comes my way – *anything.* Strangely, I seem to have long since forgotten this truth. I often see my inner life as the opposite of spacious – as confined, cramped, and filled to capacity, with only a minimal amount of extra room, and none for any more troubles! It's as if my "heart" is a physical room with walls, floors, and ceilings, and there are simply times when nothing more can be crammed into it. The fact that I glimpsed recently, and am trying to understand more fully, is that no cramming is ever necessary, because all of our hearts are as roomy and wide-open as the endless universe. There's ample room for any and all failures and misfortunes. In fact, there's so much room that I could actually *welcome* disasters when they arrive. I certainly don't have to "like" them, but I can definitely say, "Welcome. Please come in and make yourself at home." As surprising as that sounds, the fact is that welcoming adversity always makes it less scary and more able to be managed. Like a good host, I can turn those frightening visitors – the calamities that visit all of us – into relatively harmless, and even helpful, guests. I can say to misfortunes, "Now that you're here in my roomy heart, tell me what you can teach me" – and then thank them when they depart, as they always do.

⊶ ⊷

## AT THE CENTER

On our early morning kayak paddle this morning, Delycia spotted a bald eagle sitting at the top of a towering old tree. He seemed to be silently surveying his world, as though it was indeed his private property and he was proud of his possession of it. He seemed serene, like he was at the center of things and all was well with his world. Watching him as we worked our way past the tree gave me a goal to work on – to see the world as calmly and carefully as this eagle seemed to be doing. He didn't seem frenzied with a list of things to do, as I occasionally am, nor did the world seem to be an adversary with whom he struggles, but rather a sort of family, of whom he was the steadfast father. I'm part of a fairly large family, but sometimes I feel like I'm at the center of a family that's infinite, composed of eagles and lakes and continuing clouds and hills and safeguarding skies that never stop. Perhaps at those times I should sit silently, like this eagle, and simply survey the miracles that make up my world.

⊨⊰ ⊱⊨

## THE STRENGTH OF WEAKNESS

This morning I went for a peaceful float on a lake, and was surprised, as always, by the strength of the water. As I easily drifted on the surface, I wondered how something so soft can be so strong? How can water, which sometimes seems the weakest and most insubstantial of materials, easily hold up my body, to say nothing of ships of astonishing size? I suppose it has something to do with the *strength inherent in all weakness*. I once knew a man who, though bed-ridden with a paralyzing illness, radiated the rarest kind of power. To stand beside the bed of this skeletal, incapacitated man was to feel almost afloat on his joyful inner strength. And what about air, that seemingly flimsy presence all around us? Does it not sometimes sweep through our neighborhoods with incredible power, as though something fragile suddenly found the force it always had? Tomorrow, I think I'll keep a lookout for the strength in weakness – perhaps how the smallest birds soar easily across the lake, or how soft sunlight lights up an entire valley, or how old, furrowed fingers can type words that sometimes speak clearly.

⊨⊰ ⊱⊨

## A SHOW WORTH SEEING

This morning, as I was sitting on the screened porch of our cottage, the sunlight was flashing on the windswept waves of the lake, and you might say some thoughts were flashing inside me, as well. They weren't especially spectacular thoughts, just the small, unsteady, transitory thoughts that seem to be always flowing through my life. In some ways, I seem to be made mostly of thoughts. By the thousands, they stream through me each day, swirling and sometimes surging and shimmering like the ripples on the windy lake this morning. Of course, sometimes my thoughts are hushed and almost unseen, like Laurel Lake on a windless, misty day, but they're always there, these mysterious currents called thoughts, moving me through the days of my life. This morning I watched the flashing surface of the lake for a few minutes, just enjoying the ever-shifting patterns of the waves, and perhaps I should simply watch my thoughts more often. Sitting on the screened porch of my mind, I might see a fairly fascinating show.

### LEARNING FROM RAIN

Watching the rain fall today in its somewhat blasé, easygoing way, I see that it's sort of the way I'm living my life lately. I'm 74, and I guess I've done enough careful living that I can now deserve some care-free, devil-may-care days. The rain seems to sway this way and that in a totally stress-free manner, and I'm trying to let my life do something similar – lean wherever things want me to lean, swing this way or that with sorrows or joys, bend (instead of break) with the winds of change. However, being blithe about things doesn't mean being lazy or muddled, just free of the wish to control everything. The rain controls nothing, but simply sails where the weather wants it to, and I'm learning by watching. If I'm lucky, my coming days may be more like joyful free-falls than strenuous personal productions.

### FLOURISHING

While Cia's flowers are thoroughly flourishing these days, I feel like I'm doing some flourishing myself. The word comes from the

Latin *flos*, meaning "flower", and in some ways my life seems to be flowering fairly profusely in these days of my 70's. My skin may be sagging somewhat, and my days of speedy, hours-long bicycling may be over, but something keeps springing up inside me, sort of the way bulbs rise up into blossoms. Call it eagerness, or spirit, or zeal, or sparkle – whatever it is, it seems stronger than ever now that my face is furrowed with 74 years. I haven't run anywhere in years, but spirited thoughts sometimes run friskily inside me, as free as the phlox that float luxuriously in Cia's garden. My money doesn't multiply every day, but my fervent feelings definitely do – feelings that make this old life feel like the young and plentiful garden it actually is.

# MY DOMINION

I live with my wife in a small house on a small lot in a small town, but sometimes it becomes clear to me that my true home – my *dominion*, you might say – is far larger than that. The word "dominion" stems from the Latin word *domus*, meaning "home", and my real home is a vast one, stretching from the most distant stars to the deepest depths of the ocean. The truth is that, like all of us, I am an inseparable and essential part of a measureless universe. My home is not Mystic, Connecticut, USA, but the universe itself, a universe where all things, from new-born babies to massive spans of mountains, are of equal importance. We all share dominion in this dominion of ours, this universe that knows no end to its territories and provinces. From infinitesimal insects, to trees in forests, to presidents, to poor wanderers -- we're all kings and queens forever and everywhere -- if only we knew it. This morning, lucky for me, I'm knowing it.

⇒+ +⇐

## ON BEING FRESH

I was sometimes a sassy boy, causing my mother to scold me for being "fresh", and now, as a senior citizen, I'm still fresh, and feeling lucky to be so. It seems odd that "fresh" sometimes means shameless and brazen, whereas I like to think of it as meaning something new, something spotless and unused and pristine. As a boy, I guess I sometimes felt that kind of freshness as I lived the capricious and lucky life of my childhood, and I feel it more and more in these whimsical days of my retirement. I feel fresh thoughts arriving almost always. True, they sometimes can *seem* like the "same old" thoughts, but I somehow feel their freshness as they switch on their lights inside me. Each thought is as unsullied as the sunshine I see before me now, while I'm sitting outside and writing. Each feeling flows from a fresh source, no matter how old and familiar it may seem. Actually, even with my wrinkles and slumped shoulders and squeaky voice, I'm feeling fresher than ever (in an un-sassy way) and finding some fun in it. (I can see mom smiling at the news.)

## ON BEING SATISFIED

Over my 73 years, I've been fortunate to know a few people who, no matter what was happening, always seemed satisfied, and I'm continuously envious of their lucky lives. These are people who genuinely seemed at ease with wherever they were, whatever triumphs or troubles were taking place, whatever the present moment was bringing them. Almost always, they somehow seemed contented, and in a sincere way. Even in sorrow, they appeared to be what I might call comfortable, in the literal sense of being able to bring comfort to themselves. They were sad, but seemed peaceful with their sadness, calm inside their unhappiness. Whatever was happening was sufficient for them. They seemed to allow themselves to be saturated with each experience, almost as if they were easily (though perhaps not happily) swimming in it, feeling the flow of either happiness or heartache. They were – and are - a fortunate few, these contented ones, and I only hope something like their steady ease with all of life shows up in me sometime soon.

⇒+ +⇐

## RECESS

This morning, as we watched young people relaxing on the Dartmouth College green – tossing frisbees and footballs, stretching out in the sunshine, strolling hand-in-hand – it brought back memories of "recess" when I was a kid, and made we wonder if these years in my 70's have become a wholesale recess for me. The word "recess", coming from the Latin, originally meant "go back", and perhaps I've gone back, fairly wholeheartedly, to my childhood days. Perhaps I've become a born-again kid, for whom de-stressing and loosening up is an accustomed way of life. These days, I sometimes toss minutes and hours around like frisbees, just seeing how time can sail and soar when I'm not fighting it. My days are occasionally like sitting in steady sunshine, or strolling with life to see where it takes me. I still work hard, especially at reading and writing and listening and thinking and loving, but I do it like I did recess in 3rd grade. These days I skip more than I struggle.

⇒+ +⇐

## FINDING WISDOM

I guess like most of us, I have been searching for wisdom for most of my life – searching for some sense of who I am and what this thing called life is all about. Sometimes – often on silent, unblemished summer mornings like this one – I realize, to my dismay, that my search has been wasteful and silly, since true wisdom doesn't have to be searched for. It's wherever I am, as ever-present as air and as immeasurable as the sky. To find wisdom, I simply have to stop searching for it, open the door of my small, cautious self, and walk out to where boundless wisdom is always making its miracles. It's truly as simple as that.

—⟨+⟩—

## REALIZING

Occasionally I set aside an hour or so in which I do no reading or writing or walking or even talking; instead, I try to do what I call "realizing". As an alternative to prioritizing, analyzing, or drama-tizing (old habits of mine), I simply realize for a few minutes. One dictionary says to "realize" is to become fully aware of something, and to understand it better -- and this is exactly how I try to spend an hour now and then. I sometimes sit outside in the shade and do my best to realize – make more real – the limbs and leaves of trees as they bend and waver in the wind. I study them carefully and try to truly see them as they are, and before long, usually, some new understanding of them arises, as if they suddenly do become more real to me. I also sometimes realize the clouds in the summer sky above our house, just watching them wander along, steadily shift-ing their shapes. If I watch them long enough, they seem to slowly become more distinct, and therefore more remarkable, and some-how, again, a fresh kind of understanding of them comes to me. It's an instructive way to occasionally spend an hour. It's helpful, every so often, to realize this really wondrous world.

—⟨+⟩—

## HONOR AND BRIGHTNESS

I've known some people who seemed to think their lives were shameful and of no use to anyone, when all I could see radiat-ing out from them was honor and brightness. To me, they were first-class human beings who seemed to shine the light of sincere kindness wherever they were, but they seemed to see nothing but disgrace and shadows inside themselves. When I was with them, I felt lit up by their loving interest in others, by their gentleness, and by the welcoming openness of their lives, but about themselves they seemed to feel only meagerness and embarrassment. I wanted to shake them and say, "Don't you see the light of love you shine on everyone! Don't you know how wonderful you are!" Somehow, the brightness they brought to others, and the honor of their own lives – honor which helped others feel honorable as well – they never noticed.

⸛

## GETTING WISDOM

I've occasionally said to Delycia, "I'm going out to get some groceries", or "I'm going out to get the car fixed", but I'm sure I've never said, "Honey, I'm going out to get some wisdom" – and yet it's what I need the most. I devote hours and days to getting all kinds of stuff – exercise, food, money, store products, friends – but very little time getting the kind of deep understanding that brings real light to a life. I'm prompt about getting prescriptions filled, but not especially swift in getting insights about how to live with poise and light-heartedness. I'm good at getting to the Y most days for a workout, but getting wisdom about why the world sometimes seems to be in a senseless mess is another matter. I guess my priorities need repositioning. I guess getting wisdom should be right at the top, instead of down below with getting a Snickers and getting to bed at nine.

⸛

# SOFT WEAPONS

I suppose like many of us, I grew up with the idea that life is a non-stop skirmish with all kinds of enemies – hostile people, disease, disaster – and it was my task to take on these enemies with the best weapons available. Over the years, I learned to use the swords of self-deception, self-satisfaction, egotism, and a sort of concealed belligerence in wars with these so-called enemies, but in the second half of my life, I came in contact with softer weapons that seemed to work way better. I guess I learned some lessons from watching water – how its softness is what makes its astonishing strength. Water is so easy-going and graceful, and yet so forceful. It effortlessly accepts whatever falls into it, and yet is strong enough to support ships of enormous size. Slowly, my weapons – most of them, anyway – have turned into water's kind of softness, into light and mild qualities like gentleness and acceptance. I've found that calmness and hospitality can sometimes disarm the scariest enemies. In a good way, I guess I've grown soft with age.

Learning from water, my best weapon is now a sincere welcome to whatever happens. In softness I'm finding victories.

━⟨+ +⟩━

## THE INNOCENT UNIVERSE

With so much seeming disorder in the world today, it may seem silly to speak of our universe as being "innocent", and yet, when I manage to step far enough back to get a bigger picture, it truly seems like the universe does no harm, ever. Yes, there are storms and wars and heartrending losses and disasters of astonishing size, and yet the universe seems always able to stay on its steady, 15-billion-year-old course. There are tragedies, but these tragedies, again and again, seem perfectly balanced by triumphs. There's loss after loss, but the losses are always, in due course, succeeded by offsetting gains. Leaves die in autumn, but fresh life always flourishes in the spring. The universe seems to be a purely innocent and smoothly flowing river of compensation, where every wave and swell has its necessary place, and where concepts like "good" and "bad" disappear in an immense and endless harmony.

━⟨+ +⟩━

## A CHEER FOR MEEKNESS

The word "meek" has gotten an ill-deserved bad reputation, so I was happy today to find that it actually derives from the Old Norse word *"mjúkr"*, meaning "gentle". Meek people, then, are mild-mannered people, folks who live in a friendly instead of a two-fisted way. They are courageous and spirited, but in a gracious and welcoming way. They know true power comes from gentle helpfulness, not stern

251

self-centeredness. Our world could work miracles if meekness was more widespread than boastfulness.

⊫⊰ ⊱⊐

## BROKEN AND OPEN

Early this morning, as light was brightening our backyard, the phrase "break of day" came to mind, and it seemed odd that breaking something could bring good results. Here was sunshine suddenly sweeping across the yard, simply because, as we say, the day had "broken". Usually when something breaks, we think of injury or damage, but when dawn breaks, the brightness of a new day is at hand. It started me thinking of a friend who told me of the grief he suffered because of his divorce, but also of the strange rebirth he experienced. He said the break-up of his marriage brought misery, yes, but it also brought, eventually, a surprising sense of renewal – a resurgence, he said, of youthful feelings he thought were gone forever. He told me that, as the sorrow of the divorce slowly transformed into acceptance and understanding, he sometimes felt like his life was filling with light, helping him see, perhaps for the first time, who he really was. As I thought about him on this sunny morning, it seemed strange that suffering can start a new light shining -- strange that something breaking can bring to light a new and better kind of life.

⊫⊰ ⊱⊐

## GLORY IN A BACKYARD

This morning was a glorious one. Truly, all mornings are probably glorious, but this morning I was actually able to notice the glories. In just a few minutes, I saw sparrows fluttering in their simple splendor around the bird feeders, a shimmering hummingbird whirling its wings at its feeder, old and noble branches bending in the breeze, and sunlight shining on brown shingles. I must admit that I don't often notice the prestige and magnificence in our backyard, but this morning the glory couldn't be missed.

***

## OPEN WINDOWS, OPEN LIFE

Today I drove on I-95 with the car windows down, something I rarely do, and it was fun, for a change, to feel the outside world roaring into the car as I drove. It was shrill and sometimes almost harsh on my ears, but strangely, it was also sort of refreshing. It started me wondering whether I could leave the "windows" of my life open more often, just welcoming in whatever happens to come along. Could I tolerate – and even say a pleasant hello to – all the "noise" that life sends to all of us? With my "windows" – my heart –– wide open, could I learn to let in the bad with the good, and perhaps even find some wisdom and benefit in the bad? Like some of us, I drive – and live – in a fairly closed-up way, but this morning's free-feeling, open-window trip on the highway showed me the possibilities of living a more unfastened, unenclosed sort of life. It might make for a fun ride.

***

## EVENING ALL DAY

Cia and I usually have tranquil, quiet evenings, mostly at home, and it sometimes occurs to me that most of our days are actually just like these kindhearted evenings. It's interesting that the word "evening" comes from the word "even", which suggests, not the coming of night, but simply smoothness and steadiness, as in "The road ran evenly across the landscape." Maybe all our days, without our realizing it, actually run evenly along, going where they must in a level and laid-back way. Maybe we just don't notice the evenness of our days as clearly as we see the easygoing mellowness of our evenings. Perhaps we should look for the "evening" of each hour in the same way that we look forward to the quiet of our evenings at home. Maybe we can learn to see the "evening" – the smoothing out and leveling of everything – in each daytime moment.

. . . . .